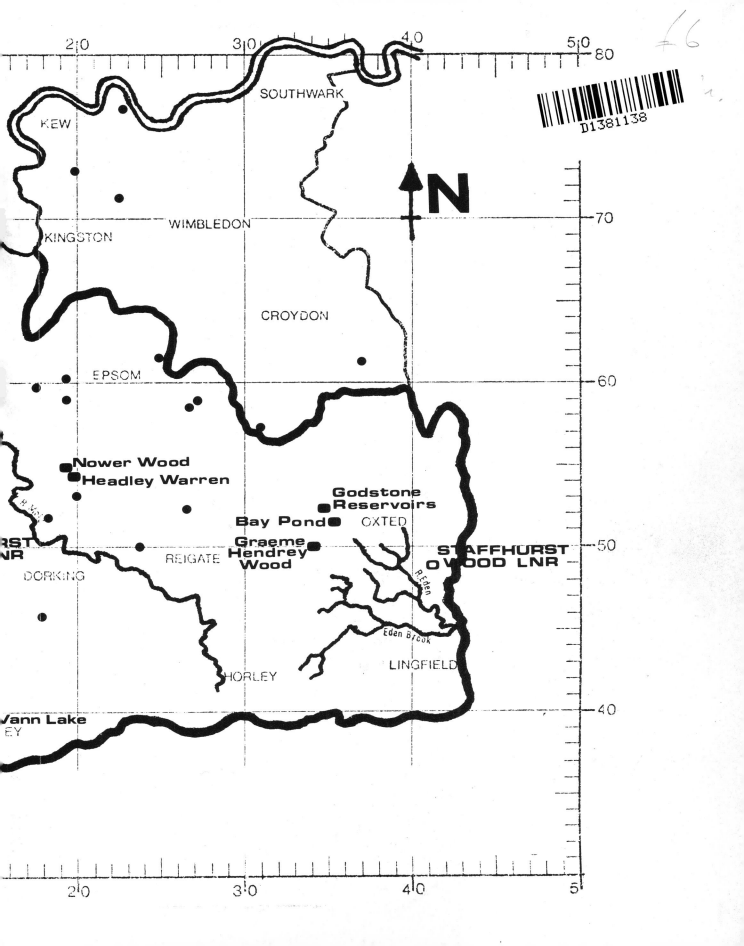

The Nature of Surrey 1987
has been published
in a Limited Edition
of which this is

Number 432

A list of original subscribers
is printed at
the back of the book

THE NATURE OF SURREY

Surrey animals. ABOVE: Fox and badger; ABOVE CENTRE: dormouse and grey squirrel; BELOW CENTRE: rabbit and roe deer; BELOW: stoat and hedgehog.

THE NATURE OF SURREY

SURREY

THE WILDLIFE AND ECOLOGY
OF THE COUNTY AND
LONDON SOUTH OF THE THAMES

BY

JOHN DREWETT

with Cover Painting and Drawings by
ROSALIE S. THOMPSON
TIM PRICE & KEITH BRANDWOOD

Photography by the author and

KEITH BETTON, ANDREW DAVIES, JERRY LOCKETT,
KEN WILMOTT & JOHN WILSON
& OTHER MEMBERS OF THE TRUST

Published with the co-operation and in aid of

SURREY WILDLIFE TRUST

FOREWORD BY DAVID BELLAMY

BARRACUDA BOOKS LIMITED
BUCKINGHAM, ENGLAND
MCMLXXXVII

THE NATURE OF BRITAIN SERIES

PUBLISHED BY BARRACUDA BOOKS LIMITED
BUCKINGHAM, ENGLAND
AND PRINTED BY
HOLYWELL PRESS LIMITED
OXFORD, ENGLAND

BOUND BY
WBC BOOKBINDERS LIMITED
MAESTEG, WALES

COLOUR PLATES AND JACKETS BY
CHENEY & SONS LIMITED
BANBURY, OXON

MONOCHROME LITHOGRAPHY BY
MRM GRAPHICS LIMITED
WINSLOW, ENGLAND

COLOUR LITHOGRAPHY BY
WESTFIELD STUDIO LIMITED
ABINGDON, ENGLAND

TYPESET IN BASKERVILLE BY
GRAHAM BURN PRODUCTIONS
LEIGHTON BUZZARD, ENGLAND

© Surrey Wildlife Trust 1987

ISBN 0 86023 247 6

Contents

List of Colour Plates

Acknowledgements

A great many people have helped in the preparation of this book, especially members of the Surrey Wildlife Trust. Deserving particular mention are the various District Officers and Reserve Wardens. Special thanks are due to John Montgomery, Humphrey Mackworth-Praed, Arthur Lindley and Ilona Billings.

I would also like to thank Ken Wilmott for information on butterflies, Adrian Davies for advice on photography, and various staff of the Nature Conservancy Council for their assistance and helpful suggestions, and Rosalie Thompson for her illustrations throughout the text. In addition Keith Betton has contributed photographs and photographic help.

Dartford warbler. (TP)

Foreword

by David Bellamy BSc, PhD, FLS

Born in London, I lived all my formative years in Surrey. I caught my first tadpoles in its ponds, learned to swim in its rivers, camped on the edge of its coppice woods and walked its highways and byways. I served part of my apprenticeship as a natural historian at Haslemere Educational Museum and was taught by the masters of the craft, John Clegg, John Sankey and Francis Rose. I discovered the delights of Youth Hostelling at the Devil's Punch Bowl, the wet wonders of bogland at Thursley and got engaged on Thors Stone in the middle of what is now a National Nature Reserve.

A Surrey naturalist, it is my honour to be a founder member and now President of the Surrey Wildlife Trust.

Surrey is a truly wonderful county which has and still offers so much to the burgeoning population of London. A lung, informal greenspace, call it what you will, Box Hill, Frensham Ponds, Leith Hill, The Weald, Hindhead and many others still attract visitors in their millions each year and yet they are still habitats for some of our rarer and most fascinating flora and fauna. Then there are the more secret places, Sites of Special Scientific Interest, well managed farmscapes, hedgerows, copses, roadside verges, ponds, meanders in rivers and streams, tiny waterfalls, springs, old quarries which have changed little since I was a boy. These are all key sites for our wildlife and the stock-in-trade of the Wildlife Trust.

Please read this smashing book, learn more about our wonderful county, why it is like it is, how it ticks and what is needed to keep it ticking.

Then if you are a member of the Trust, roll up your sleeves and get down to work. If you are not, then join today.

Key to Caption Credits

KB	Keith Betton	RS	Raven Studios
DAE	D.A. Edwardson	KBR	Keith Brandwood
FG	Frank Greenaway	JEGM	J.E.G. Morris
RST	Rosalie S. Thompson	BMS	B.M. Spicer
		TP	Tim Price

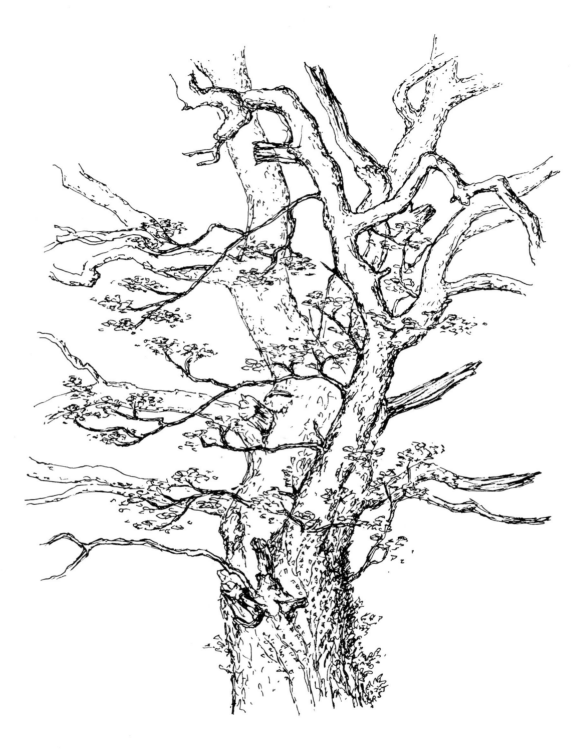

Oak with mosses. (RST)

Genesis

Today, there is little relationship between natural features and the Surrey county boundary. In the west, it partly follows the river Blackwater. To the north, the border was once formed by the Thames, a river that now flows through Surrey. Large parts of the county have, at various times been engulfed by London. No other county, with the exception of Middlesex, has suffered so much at the hands of the capital. The remnants of Middlesex, around Staines and Ashford, were transferred to Surrey in 1965. Finally, whilst a length of the eastern boundary follows a Roman road, much of the border with Kent and Sussex meanders between a selection of Wealden villages.

This book deals with the present-day administrative county of Surrey, plus the London boroughs of Richmond, Kingston, Sutton, Merton and Croydon. This is the area in which the Surrey Wildlife Trust operates. Within it live about two million people, the largest proportion in the heavily developed northern part.

Although the area covered by Surrey has been occupied by Man since at least Mesolithic times (8,000 to 4,000 BC) when a site at Abinger was used, it does not appear to have been of major importance until recent centuries.

Long before Man came on the scene, geological processes had begun to mould the Surrey landscape.

It was about 25m years ago, during the period of mountain building when the Alps were formed, that a range of rocks already laid down over what is now southern England, were folded into a dome. These rocks had been deposited over the previous 100m years as sediments in both marine and fresh water.

Subsequent erosion of this dome, the development of river systems, and some modification during the Ice Ages, have left the edges of these sedimentary layers exposed. Thus, formations of different rocks run roughly east to west across the county, in a series of relatively narrow bands. There are, of course, anomalies, but the general rule is that anyone travelling north to south across Surrey will quickly cross at least seven geological formations. Because of this variety, and the effect different soil types had on early agriculture, parishes tend to be long and narrow, running north-south, thereby sharing out the different strata fairly.

The oldest rocks to reach the surface in Surrey are the Tunbridge Wells sands. These were deposited in a large delta, which formed on the northern side of a Wealden lake, 125m years ago. The fauna of the area at the time would have been rich, yet the deposits have not produced any notable fossils. Tunbridge Wells sands are only visible in the extreme south-east of the county.

A little younger in age is the Weald Clay, which forms a broad band across the southern part of the county. This low-lying deposit is believed to have been formed when hills to the north were eroded. It contains a variety of materials, including shales, mudstones and shelly limestones. The most important outcrop of bedded stone in this region is a form of sandstone known as Horsham Stone. Rather alkaline in nature, it was often used to roof cottages and churches, near the Sussex border. Shelly, or Paludina limestone outcrops intermittently throughout the Weald Clay, locally affecting the flora.

The Weald Clay is both heavily farmed and heavily wooded. Prairie farming has not developed here yet, many of the fields having been cut directly from the woodland. Although some crops are grown, much permanent pasture exists, providing grazing for cattle. Ploughing such heavy soils is not easy. In some areas, particularly south of Dorking, the clay is used for brickmaking. Specialist handmade tiles are produced near Cranleigh.

There is a sharp contrast between the Weald Clay and the next formation to the north, Lower Greensand. At the end of the period during which Weald Clay was laid down, the Wealden lake increased its link with the sea, becoming a shallow marine bay.

Lower Greensand is actually a combination of four main strata. Oldest to youngest, these are Atherfield Clay, Hythe Beds, Sandgate and Bargate Beds, and Folkestone Beds. The formations follow a narrow band in the east of the county, which broadens considerably beyond Dorking, giving rise to extensive heathlands in western Surrey.

Some of the most spectacular scenery in Surrey is due to Lower Greensand. South-west of Dorking are four major hills called Leith Hill, Holmbury Hill, Pitch Hill and Winterfold Heath. This is the highest area in the Weald. At 294m, Leith Hill is the highest point in south-east England. These escarpments are effectively the Hythe Beds, which are capped with chert, a hard layer which considerably reduces erosion. The upper part of these hills is steep, the slope becoming more gentle at the junction of the Atherfield Clay. A line of springs surrounds the hill at this point, leading to a marshy belt just a few metres wide, but several kilometres long.

Above Chilworth, St Martha's Hill appears to be similar, but its highest part is formed of Folkestone Beds. This gives the impression of a high hill made of soft sands. However, carstone, a hard bed, is irregularly dispersed throughout the Folkestone Beds, thereby capping the hill.

Near Hindhead, the A3 Portsmouth Road follows the rim of a deep valley known as the Devil's Punchbowl. Here, a stream has cut through the Hythe Beds to the Atherfield Clay, forming steep slopes. To the north, the Atherfield Clay goes underground, and the spring line disappears. The subsequent undermining of the valley head has caused considerable enlargement, forming the Punchbowl.

The Lower Greensand formations also have a certain economic value. Today, the greatest use is for high quality sands, especially between Dorking and Godstone. Around Nutfield, Fuller's Earth is also quarried. These workings are all opencast. Many exhausted quarries have been infilled with rubbish, but several still remain, lending a somewhat derelict air to parts of the area. In Dorking, parts of the town have been built in and around the old quarries. Until recent years, when their numbers were severely reduced by increasing desertification in Africa, sand martins nested extensively here. Hard stone from these formations was once quarried for roadstone in the area now managed as the Graeme Hendrey Reserve on Tilburstow Hill.

Along the foot of the North Downs are two narrow bands formed by Gault and Upper Greensand. The former was probably laid down in still water, away from the source of sediment. Upper Greensand was more likely deposited in shallow, coastal conditions. Gault appears to have a rich fauna in which mollusc fossils predominate.

Some of the sandstones forming part of the Upper Greensand have been mined in Surrey. Around Reigate, malmstone was mined for building material, and to line furnaces, where it gained the name firestone. A different variety, known as hearthstone, was used to whiten hearths. All these mines are now disused. Some are important for bats.

One of the best known features of Surrey are the North Downs, probably because of such excellent viewpoints as Box Hill. The ridge, which runs from Farnham to Dover, effectively divides Surrey in two. The area to the north is mostly heavily developed, that to the south more rural. The southern slopes are generally steep, warm and sunny, whilst the cooler north-facing ones slope gently down to the London Clay. An exception to this is the Hog's Back, between Farnham and Guildford, where the rocks are faulted. This has produced a narrow ridge, with steep drops to both sides.

Rivers break through the North Downs in only two places in the county. At Guildford, the River Wey forms a steep-sided valley through the chalk. The valley of the River Mole is wider, but still steep, especially where it passes below Box Hill, forming a spectacular river cliff known as The Whites. The woodlands clothing these precipitous slopes must be the least affected by Man in Surrey, due to the difficulty of access.

In several places along the Downs, quarrying has taken place. Some of these workings, such as Seale Chalk Pit, were small and inconspicuous, but others, like the Brockham and Betchworth quarries, have left major scars on the hillsides, visible from a great distance. Only at Oxted can a working quarry be found today. Seale is a Surrey Wildlife Trust reserve, and Brockham a public open space.

In places, the northern dip slope of the Downs is broken up by a series of dry valleys. These are particularly noticeable on Headley Heath and Box Hill. They are believed to have been formed when the meltwater from Ice Age snowfields ran over the frozen surface.

Chalk itself is a fairly permeable rock comprising over 95% calcium carbonate. It was largely formed about 65m years ago from microscopic skeletal remains of coccoliths which were probably derived from the simple aquatic plants like algae. In most places, the tops of the Downs support a selection of plants such as bracken, which prefers acid conditions. This is possible, due to a later capping of clay-with-flints. The flints from this layer are sometimes used for building, as can be seen at Ranmore.

The north of the county is covered by the two most recent geological formations, London Clay and Bagshot Beds. A large proportion of London Clay has now been built over, but where it remains undeveloped supports grassy commons and oak woodland. Examples occur at Ashtead, Epsom and Bookham, where the ground frequently becomes waterlogged in winter.

The fine, buff-coloured sands and flint pebbles of the Bagshot Beds give rise to the wild, open heathlands of north-west Surrey. Many areas are used for military training, but extensive areas are also open to the public. Whether public or military, these areas are rich in wildlife. Often seen as wasteland, the large blocks of Surrey heathland are of tremendous importance.

There are many other variations in the geology of Surrey, but the foregoing is a general outline. Although geology is overlooked by many people, the plants growing on the surface give important clues to the rocks found beneath.

ABOVE: Wealden deciduous woodland, near Haslemere. (KB) BELOW:
Beech woodland, Box Hill. (KB)

14

Woodlands

One of the most obvious features of the Surrey landscape is the preponderance of trees. The county probably has more trees per hectare than any other. A patchwork of woodland extends to all corners of the county which, when seen from some prominent hilltop, appears more dense than it really is. If Man had not interfered, the natural vegetation would have been almost entirely woodland.

Forestry Commission data indicates that some 19% of Surrey is wooded, that is, about 31,500 hectares (78,750 acres). Conifer woodland probably makes up about 25% of this area. Another one-fifth is best described as scrub. The rest, approximately half, can be said to be deciduous of some sort.

Over the centuries, the natural climax vegetation has been modified by Man cutting, clearing and replanting the woods. Fields and heathlands now exist where once would have been mainly oak woodland. Growing among the oaks would have been lesser numbers of beech, ash, yew, juniper, box and other native species.

Ironworking has been known in the Weald for over 2,000 years. During its height, much woodland must have been felled for charcoal production. In addition, many woods were grazed. On the greensand hills in central Surrey, the combination of grazing and cutting the wood for charcoal effectively destroyed the trees by the 19th century. Then much planting took place by people such as Evelyn.

Many of the woods today exhibit foreign trees introduced by Man. Sweet chestnut and sycamore are just two out of hundreds of introduced species. It is the native trees, however, which are of special value to wildlife. Over the thousands of years they have existed in Britain, numerous species of insects, fungi, mosses and lichens have adapted to them, thereby producing food for woodland birds and mammals.

No woodlands in Surrey, and probably few in Britain, can claim to be unaffected by Man in some way. The least affected in Surrey are probably the box and yew woods, which cling precariously to the river cliff above the Mole at Box Hill. Although minor paths provide some access, this is limited by the precipitous slopes.

Box Hill was named after its groves of wild box trees, which grow naturally in only a few places in Britain. One theory suggests they were once more widespread, but have been reduced in numbers following exploitation for their extremely hard wood, used for mathematical instruments. Another is that they were introduced by the Romans, with whom they seem to have been popular.

Table 1

Approximate percentage cover of dominant tree species in Surrey woods (based on Forestry Commission Census, 1980).

*Oak (Pedunculate/Sessile)	21%	Corsican pine	2.5%
*Birch	18%	Japanese/hybrid larch	2%
Scots Pine	16%	Douglas fir	2%
*Mixed broadleaves	8%	European larch	1.5%
*Beech	8%	Sycamore	1.5%
*Ash	5.5%	*Poplar	1.5%
Norway spruce	3%	Mixed conifers	1%
*Other broadleaves	3%	Sitka spruce/lodgepole pine	0.4%
Sweet chestnut	2.5%	*Elm	0.1%
Other conifers	2.5%	*Native species, or including native species	

Box does not grow to a great size, and is often twisted and snake-like. An evergreen, with small, leathery leaves, it is only found on chalk in the wild.

Apart from its own rarity value, box supports several specialist invertebrates. A spider, *Hyptiotes paradoxus,* is confined to box and yew. It has been found only in two other places in Britain. Two other spiders, *Diaea dorsata* and *Theridion tinctum* also have a distinct preference for these two trees.

Yew not only grows alongside box, but is widely distributed across Surrey, sometimes forming pure stands on the chalk. On greensand, it grows mainly as an isolated tree in mixed woodland. A preference for well-drained soils is the cause of its virtual absence from the clays.

Druid's Grove in Norbury Park is an excellent example of old yew woodland. The trees are massive in both age and proportions, and prevent most light reaching the ground. Consequently, there is an absence of vegetation beneath. Another spider, *Hybocoptus decoliatus,* is confined to yew, except on the coast, where it lives on gorse. This species has also been recorded at Box Hill.

Box and yew woods are often quiet, few birds penetrating beneath the canopy. Yew is the more popular, especially for its berries. Small woodland birds like tits and robins may be seen amid the trees, searching for insects. Being relatively undisturbed, such woods often provide excellent sites for badger setts. These can be found surprisingly close together, and may be identified by the large mounds of excavated soil, well worn tracks, latrine pits and discarded bedding.

Badgers are rather common in the chalk country, often excavating large pieces of rock whilst digging their setts. They are also found in sandy areas to some extent, so long as the rock is hard enough to prevent the collapse of their tunnels.

A rare tree of the chalk is juniper. Placenames provide evidence of the former abundance of this species, which is now restricted to a few plants in a few localities. None of these can be described as real woodland, although juniper does sometimes grow in association with other species. The largest colony is at Hackhurst Downs, near Gomshall. Two rare moths restricted to this tree have been recorded from Surrey, namely the juniper pug and juniper carpet.

Another characteristic chalk tree is the beech. The species also grows well on clay-with-flints capping the chalk, and on lower greensand. Elsewhere, it is scattered throughout the county, although in many locations, it must have been planted.

Perhaps the most visually spectacular type of beechwood is the so-called 'hanger'. This is a steep hillside on which large beeches make an almost pure stand. There are many examples in the county, the best being at Norbury Park, Marden Park, Netley Park and alongside the lane from Juniper Hall to Headley.

Like yew, beech prevents most light from reaching the ground, thereby preventing the majority of plants from growing. They do, however, provide a home for several interesting and characteristic species, including bird's-nest orchid, yellow bird's-nest and green hound's tongue. The first two are quite similar. Being brown in colour, they are difficult to spot among the carpet of dead leaves from which they obtain nourishment. Green hound's tongue is extremely rare, but has been recorded from the Mickleham area for more than 300 years.

Many fungi are particularly associated with beechwoods, especially those of the genera *Cortinarius, Marasmius* and *Russula. Oudemansiella mucida* is a slimy, white fungus which grows on the wood itself.

Off the chalk, the bird's-nest orchid and yellow bird's-nest may sometimes be found growing in lesser numbers. These are subject to wide fluctuations, so are difficult to find. Likewise, other species of orchid may grow under beech, depending on the available light.

On the clay-with-flints, atop the Downs, beech may be found but, with greater numbers of other trees, particularly pedunculate oak and ash. Such woods are inclined to contain grassy glades and patches of bracken. These open areas are important for plants, insects, birds, mammals and reptiles. Most species found in woodland live close to the edge. Glades can be considered extensions of the edge.

Obviously, the longer a wood exists, the greater the chance of additional species moving in. From a conservation viewpoint, the greater the diversity of species, the better. Land which has been continuously wooded since at least 1600 is known as Ancient Woodland. This does not mean that Man has not removed timber or managed it in any way during that time. The earliest record of woodland generally available in Surrey is a map by Rocque, pre-1762. This indicates that several of the woods found today in the Weald existed at that time. A particularly fine group occurs around Chiddingfold, and extends into Sussex. Some woods in other parts of the county are also shown, such as Great Hurst Wood, between Headley and Walton-on-the-Hill.

Most of these Ancient Woodlands have been exploited in the past for timber of various sorts. Frequently, this was done on a coppice-with-standards basis.

Deciduous trees, if cut down to near ground level, sprout new shoots the following year. Where there was once one stem, several grow. If a block of woodland is cut this way, clearing a section each year over a period of seven to fourteen years, a supply of poles is guaranteed, which can be used for fencing, tool handles and so on. Generally, most of the coppice in a wood is of one species, often hazel or sweet chestnut. However, the species will depend on the uses to which it was put, and the underlying soil type. Between the clumps, or stools as they are known, trees were planted at fairly wide intervals to provide a future supply of large timber. Often oak was used for this purpose.

Unwittingly, this form of management brought great benefits to nature. The increased light resulting from coppicing encourages woodland flowers like bluebells, primrose, wood anemone and wood sorrel. These attract large numbers of insects, which in turn attract other creatures. As the coppice regrows, the bushy growth is ideal for birds to nest in. Slowly, the flowers are shaded out, then the growth becomes too straight for nest sites. By this time, the cycle is ready to start again.

Alas, this type of management is now a thing of the past. Farmers have abandoned cutting the timber, which kept their employees busy during the winter, and now buy the products ready-made. Many of the Wealden woods have consequently grown dense and dark, all trace of the ground flora gone.

More recently groups of volunteers have restarted coppicing in several parts of the county. Often this has been on nature reserves. Usually, it has met with success, but in some cases high numbers of roe deer have prevented the regrowth of shoots from the coppice stools.

Roe deer are common throughout the county. They prefer woods with plenty of vegetation, or young plantations, in which they lay up during the day. Small parties may build up during the winter, but usually they are to be found singly or in pairs. Sometimes they may be seen browsing during the day in quiet woods. Territories are vigorously defended, and marked by fraying the bark of trees. Additionally, fraying occurs when the bucks remove the dead skin, or velvet, from their antlers in spring. Apart from fraying and footprints, the other main sign of a deer's presence in a wood is an area of flattened vegetation used as a sleeping place.

Roe deer feed on a variety of leaves, berries or fungi, and have a particular preference for bramble and wild roses. The ends of shoots show a distinctive fray.

Where roe deer have not prevented regrowth of coppice, the variety of different aged blocks leads to a fascinating and attractive range of wildlife. One species which may repay careful searching in this habitat is the dormouse, which feeds on the fruits of many shrubs, including hazel.

At Wallis Wood, a SWT reserve, a complete cycle of coppicing has now been established. A rich ground flora has developed, including sheets of bluebells. Other plants include broad-leaved helleborine orchid, primrose, wood anemone, wood sorrel and violet helleborine. A patch of wild daffodil also flowers in the reserve. This is rather a rare plant in Surrey, being confined to the Weald clay.

In some Wealden coppice-with-standards woods, both the pedunculate and sessile oak grow. In addition, ash, hornbeam, wild cherry, wild service tree, midland hawthorn and crab apple are found. Sessile oak grows largely in the south and east of Surrey, usually on acid soils. Banstead Wood is the largest sessile oakwood in the county. Hornbeam is believed to be native on the Weald clay, but possibly introduced elsewhere. Wild service tree is rather rare in Surrey, and confined to the Weald clay. In some places it has undoubtedly been planted, and is a feature of two SWT reserves at Vann Lake and Wallis Wood.

Steep-sided streams are fairly characteristic of the Wealden woods. The areas alongside these gills (or ghylls) are frequently of special interest as they are likely to have supported the most continuous woodland cover. The steep slopes make past clearance less likely. Parts of Glovers Wood, near Charlwood are a good example of this. Here a selection of hornbeam coppice with ash, wych elm, field maple, hazel and small-leaved lime fills the valley of the Welland Gill. Small-leaved lime may be native here, but has also been planted in other woods, where rings of the tree may sometimes be seen. Large-leaved lime is also planted in a few localities, but is generally rare. Common lime, a cross between the two, is planted and naturalised throughout the county.

Yellow archangel and dog's mercury are characteristic components of the ground flora in Wealden woods, as in others which have been largely undisturbed. The plateau above the Welland Gill is woodland which was developed last century over old fields. This is believed to have happened in a number of other sites in the county, both by planting and natural regeneration.

Damp woodlands are also more likely to be old-established, as planting would have been difficult, or uneconomic, in these conditions. Alder is the most common tree found in waterlogged soil. Redpolls often frequent such woods. Characteristic plants include marsh marigold and bladder sedge. Examples of alder carr may be found at Bay Pond and Moor Park reserves.

The variety of plants of the Weald clay woods gives rise to a wide range of insects, especially butterflies. Speckled wood butterflies, frequent throughout the county, are abundant in good summers, flying in the dappled shade and laying their eggs on various grasses. Occurring frequently, though rarely seen, is the magnificent purple emperor. Binoculars are useful to spot this large butterfly which flies around treetops in July and August. Its larval foodplants are various willows, especially sallow.

Since the Second World War, two fritillaries have been lost to the Wealden woods. The marsh fritillary and high brown fritillary have not been seen for many years now, whilst the pearl bordered fritillary and silver washed fritillary have suffered reduced numbers. Both these last two

Roe deer

species feed on violets, which are still widespread in Surrey woods, so offer no clues as to the reasons for the contraction in their range.

One butterfly which has staged a major comeback since 1969, is the wood white. The comma is also frequent, as is the white admiral. The white admiral depends very much on the presence of its foodplant, honeysuckle. Although honeysuckle harms trees by winding itself tightly around the trunk, it is frequently left in nature reserves, for the benefit of these butterflies. White-letter hairstreaks have largely disappeared following the virtual elimination of their foodplant elm, by disease. The brown hairstreak, however, is still regularly reported, although its foodplant, blackthorn, is declining. In some places, dense impenetrable blackthorn thickets still occur in woods, but many have been cleared in tidying-up schemes. In other places, like Vann Lake, careful management aims to encourage development of such thickets.

The lime hawk moth is reasonably well distributed, and sometimes common in the London and Surrey areas. The main foods of the caterpillars are the various limes, although alder, silver birch and several other trees are known to have been eaten. Until its demise, elm was also a favoured species.

The mixed deciduous woods of the Weald, and several other parts of the county, are home to a variety of other large moths.

Caterpillars of the poplar hawk moth may be found on the leaves of grey poplar, aspen and sallow, from July to September. On occasions, they may even persist into October, before pupating. The pupae overwinter below ground, but close to the surface. The commonest of our hawkmoths, this species is on the wing from May to August.

A pale brown moth known as the double square spot, is named after the dark marks on its forewings. Found in most woods, its larvae feed on silver birch, hawthorn, blackthorn, bramble, sallow and various docks. A related, but far less common species, the triple-spotted clay, has also been recorded from some woods, where it feeds on a range of plants including dandelion, primrose and various chickweeds.

Frequently found in Surrey woods is the white marked moth. Hibernating as a chrysalis, it flies around sallow catkins in the spring. Sallow is one of the caterpillar foodplants; another is bilberry. Consequently, this species may be encountered over a wider range of woods than some others.

A variety of trees support the brown caterpillar of the nut-tree tussock. Not surprisingly, one of these is hazel, but the larvae, of which there are two generations, also consume the leaves of beech, birch and hornbeam.

Widely distributed is the aptly named winter moth. Feeding on a variety of trees, the larvae eventually metamorphose into brownish moths, which are on the wing between October and February. Another brown moth, the drab looper, feeds on wood spurge, so may be expected in some woods where this plant makes up a substantial proportion of the ground flora.

When trees appear to be defoliated in May, this may be due to the larvae of the mottled umber, which can occur in enormous numbers. As well as consuming the leaves of birch, oak and many other trees, it can also attack dog rose and honeysuckle.

Where pedunculate oak is the dominant tree, several other moths may be present. Among these are the great prominent, oak hook-tip, oak beauty, great oak beauty and festoon moths. The oak hook-tip is rather uncommon, rarely discovered except when using light traps. One site it does frequent is Holmwood Common, near Dorking. The oak beauty is uncommon, but widespread, whilst the great oak beauty has turned up from some locations, including woodland at Westcott.

The greensand woods present a totally different aspect to those of the claylands to the south. The acidity of the soil encourages several plants not found, or less common, elsewhere. Some of these can reach pest proportions, reducing the variety of ground flora present.

Bracken can take over extensive areas. Various methods of control have been tried, including regular cutting, digging the plants up, or spraying with Asulox, a chemical specific to bracken. All are successful to varying degrees, the best method depending on the size of the area to be treated.

Another serious pest is rhododendron. All over the lower greensand, and elsewhere where the soil has an acidic tendency, this naturalised garden escape is well established. Much of its spread seems to have taken place this century. Now it reaches tree proportions in many areas, its dense evergreen shade eliminating all plants beneath. A certain amount of clearing has taken place in recent years, but it is a difficult plant to eradicate, being little affected by herbicides, and freely seeding in the wild. Like many introduced species, it supports little wildlife, its main consumer being a leafhopper, *Graphocephala coccinea,* itself an accidental introduction from North America.

20

Other species are a pest in woods on both greensand and other soils. One of the most widespread of these is the sycamore. Originally introduced from the Mediterranean, the sycamore spread rapidly through Surrey during the first half of the 19th century, swamping many woods. It takes advantage of any gaps in the canopy, such as those caused by fallen trees, quickly taking over. It is particularly prevalent on disturbed ground, such as the Graeme Hendrey reserve at Bletchingley, which was once quarried for stone. Here, it has densely colonised the disturbed areas, yet only odd trees have moved into the rest of the wood. Sycamore is home to enormous quantities of insects, mainly aphids, but also supports the sycamore moth.

The Graeme Hendrey reserve is particularly interesting as a woodland due to its geology. Parts of the Hythe beds have been quarried, the rest being shown on the geological map as 'head'. This is generally considered to be a disturbed and unsorted mass of rock formed under tundra conditions, during the Ice Ages. This is evident by the juxtaposition of species like dogwood and bracken, which generally prefer rather different levels of acidity.

The reserve supports a wide range of herbaceous plants. These include bird's-nest orchid, bitter vetch, broad-leaved helleborine, early purple orchid, moschatel, tutsan, wood sanicle, wood speedwell, and yellow pimpernel. None of these are necessarily confined to the greensand, and none are particularly rare, but several prefer damp woods such as are found at Graeme Hendrey, particularly in the old quarry bottoms.

LEFT: Wild primrose (RST); RIGHT: stag beetle (KBR)

The humidity of the wooded quarries makes the reserve especially important for ferns and mosses too. Ferns recorded include bracken, hard shield fern, soft shield fern, adder's tongue, broad buckler fern, male fern, hard fern, hart's tongue, and lady fern. Both the hard and soft shield ferns are only found in scattered localities in Surrey. Adder's tongue is more usually found in grassland, whilst hard fern is confined to acid soils, mostly in the west of the county. Hart's tongue, characterised by wide strap-like leaves, is widely distributed in Surrey, but only in a few places does it grow in its natural woodland habitat.

Perhaps some of our most primitive plants are the horsetails, three of which grow at Graeme Hendrey. These simple plants, with central stems and spirally arranged leaves, are reminders of the type of vegetation growing in Surrey when the dinosaurs ruled the Earth. As its name implies, the common horsetail is widely distributed throughout the county, frequently outside woods. Great horsetail is less common, but prefers damp, shady places, whilst the wood horsetail is local, otherwise being confined to the south-west of Surrey. Another rare relative of the ferns, stagshorn clubmoss, is mainly confined to the area around Leith Hill, where it puts in the occasional appearance along Forestry Commission rides.

The greensand woods of the Leith Hill area are different from any others in Surrey. Although large blocks of deciduous woodland occur, there are extensive areas of conifers too. Some are under private ownership, whilst others are managed by the Forestry Commission. The total block of woodland is extensive, covering Hurtwood, Winterfold Heath, Holmbury Hill and Pitch Hill. It is at a high altitude compared to the rest of Surrey, and has a shrub layer largely composed of ling and bilberry. Common wintergreen, rare in the county, grows here and in the heathy woods to the west. There is also a small colony near Bletchingley.

In western Surrey, much heathland has been invaded by trees over recent years. This followed the cessation of common grazing and the subsequent outbreak, in the 1950s, of myxamatosis. Although some of these new woods are largely birch, much is made up of Scots pine. In places, the original heathland vegetation has died out, leaving almost pure pine woodland. Where the invasion took place some time ago, there is little to be gained by attempting to regain the heathland, although selective thinning could bring about a more varied age structure. Although generally believed to be an introduced species, Scots pine may once have been native in Surrey. John Evelyn is said to have been the first to plant Scots pine, which became popular along with other evergreens.

In other areas, such as Headley Heath, birch has been the main invasive species. Generally a pioneer tree, it is slowly replaced by others as time goes by. In some parts of the heath, oak is now developing well. The lighter shade cast by birch trees often allows ling to continue for a considerable time beneath. In winter, flocks of redpoll and siskin may be seen feeding on the catkins of birch, sometimes associating with goldfinches.

Birch is a good indicator of woodland which has been disturbed, cleared or badly managed. Parts of the Nower Wood reserve show extensive areas of this species, particularly where Canadian soldiers were stationed during the war.

Birch and pinewoods both have their characteristic associated fungi. The birch bracket fungus is ubiquitious on that species, whilst the fly agaric frequently grows beneath these trees. The latter is the red and white spotted toadstool often illustrated in children's books, although it is poisonous.

Birch woods support a series of specialist moth species. One, the northern winter moth, was once thought to be restricted to northern Britain but is now known to be widespread in Surrey. The grey birch moth is much commoner in the south than elsewhere in Britain. Here it may be found on alder as well as birch. Well known from the Dorking, Weybridge and Haslemere areas for some years, is the scarce prominent, which lays its pale blue eggs on the underside of birch leaves during April and May.

The caterpillar of the common lutestring may be found feeding on birch leaves between August and October. It uses silk to spin the leaves together for shelter during the day, coming out to feed only at night. In addition, it has also been recorded feeding on oak, alder and hazel.

Yellow-horned moth caterpillars prefer the younger birch bushes to mature trees. They feed in mid summer, folding the leaf neatly in half for protection. It pupates during the autumn, just below the soil surface, usually emerging the following spring. Some pupae, however, spend two winters below ground before emerging. Also widespread in Surrey birch woods are the colourful orange underwing and large emerald moths.

Some birds, like the willow warbler, have benefitted from this invasive woodland. Other woodland birds, such as the wood warbler, are more selective in their choice of habitat. The least common of the leaf warblers in the county, it prefers open woodland with only a thin covering of ground vegetation. Although widespread in Surrey, it is very local in its distribution. Commonest along the greensand hills, where it is mostly associated with bilberry-dominated ground vegetation, it also lives in woods on the North Downs and on some of the wooded commons like Ashtead and Bookham. Numbers seem to vary considerably, but wood warblers are generally commonest around Haslemere.

Other warblers encountered in Surrey woods are the chiffchaff and blackcap which are both regular visitors to many areas each summer. Our smallest bird, the goldcrest, is also common, both in deciduous and coniferous woods.

All three woodpeckers are found in the county, but the great spotted is the commonest woodland species. Green woodpeckers are often heard in woods, and need them for nesting, but may also be seen raiding ant hills on the Downs. Lesser spotted woodpeckers, being smaller, are less easily seen, but are probably rarer too. Some localities support all three species.

Old trees provide holes in which many species nest. Among these may be included the tits (blue, great, coal, marsh and willow), the nuthatch, and even mandarin duck. Nuthatches generally choose holes that are slightly too big, plastering up the entrance with mud, until it is just the right size. Mandarin duck, a colourful introduced species from China, may often nest in tree holes some considerable distance from water.

A game bird characteristic of many Surrey woods is the woodcock. A wader, it needs wet areas for feeding, whilst requiring dry ground for nesting. At dusk, it performs an advertisement flight called roding, during which a squeaking and croaking call are made. Whilst roding, wing beats are slow and deliberate, like those of an owl. Woods with wide rides and glades are typical habitat. Although the symbol of Nower Wood, it is found throughout the county.

Pesticides were responsible for reducing populations of the sparrowhawk even more than gamekeepers in the past. However, despite being considered a major predator of pheasants, the sparrowhawk is a relatively common woodland raptor. Among other birds of prey inhabiting Surrey woods, tawny owl and kestrel are the more usual.

Other birds have rather specialist requirements. Treecreepers need trees with some loose bark so they can nest behind it. Crossbills are adapted to feeding on pine cones, so are likely to increase if conifer woodland spreads. Some, like the hawfinch, need trees which produce large seeds, such as hornbeam, beech and wild cherry. They are probably widely, if thinly, spread across Surrey, but are seldom seen due to their shy nature.

In many parts of Surrey, woodland trees have either reached, or passed, maturity. Whilst some have been left to their own devices, other areas have been felled and replanted. Where old trees are felled, this has not only reduced the habitat available for fungi and insects, but also for hole-nesting birds. Nestboxes have been erected in some places, including Nower Wood at Headley, and Perrots Wood, Banstead. These provide nesting sites for blue tits and similar small birds. Others, like redstarts, are more affected by felling. They are believed to have declined in recent years.

Another group of creatures for which old trees with holes and loose bark are important, are the bats. Little is known of their lifestyle or distribution. The pipistrelle bat is the commonest, but other recorded species in Surrey include the whiskered, natterer's, serotine, Leisler's, and noctule bats. All of these are believed to use holes or crevices in trees, either during summer or winter.

In some parts of the county, agriculture has progressed at the expense of woodlands. Many of the Wealden fields were cut directly from the wood, leaving narrow strips of woodland, known as shaws, between fields. However, many woods have survived as pheasant copses, particularly in areas where shooting is important. Today, the biggest threats facing broadleaved woodland in Surrey are possible conversion to conifers, and a serious lack of active management.

ABOVE: Ancient oak trees on Ashtead Common. BELOW: Scots pine
woodland, Thursley Common. (KB)

ABOVE: Birch woodland at Barfold Copse, Haslemere, with an under-
storey of bracken and holly and BELOW: after thinning and clearance.
(KB)

ABOVE: Mature alder woodland, alongside the river Mole, Betchworth.
(KB) BELOW: Recently coppiced woodland, Wallis Wood. (KB)

LEFT: Fifth year coppice regrowth, Wallis Wood. RIGHT: Sunny woodland glade suitable for flowers and butterflies. BELOW: Young pine plantation in an area formerly of oak, Friday Street. (KB)

LEFT: Even aged invasive woodland, Headley Heath. RIGHT: Leaf of wild service tree. (RS) BELOW: Old yew woodland, now dead, but still surrounded by little vegetation, ideal for a badger sett. (KB)

LEFT: Female roe deer (RS); RIGHT: buff tip moth (*Phalara bucephala*) (DAE)
and BELOW: pipistrelle bat. (DAE)

LEFT: Convolvulus (RST) and RIGHT: broad-leaved helleborine. (DAE) BELOW: Marsh fritillaries – long gone from Surrey woodlands. (DAE)

Grasslands

After woodland, it is probably the chalk grassland of the North Downs which is the most characteristic feature of Surrey. As broad-leaved woodland is the native vegetation, this must have been created by Man.

Before the Neolithic period, any human occupation of the county would have been mainly by hunter-gatherers. These would have cleared few trees other than for their immediate needs. Neolithic Man, on the other hand, introduced agriculture, so was probably responsible for the first real grasslands. These early clearances would have been made on the hilltops and poorer soils, for it was there that tree cover was thinnest.

Surprisingly, it is the poor quality of the soil that is responsible for the tremendous interest of chalk grassland. Without the nutrients found in other soils, most plants are unable to grow much. Coupled with the fact that many plants can tolerate, or even require, a calcium-rich soil, this has led to the development of a sward comprising a tremendous variety of relatively small plants, which do not compete significantly for light. Consequently, chalk grassland is one of the richest botanical habitats. The plants are attractive to insects too, which particularly enjoy the warm slopes of the south-facing Downs.

Traditionally, downland was kept open by the grazing of livestock, largely sheep. Much of that ceased earlier this century for economic reasons. In places, downland turf was ploughed up for grain production, whilst in others, agriculture on the Downs was abandoned to some extent. Once myxamatosis decimated the rabbit population in the 1950s, hawthorn, dogwood, ash and other invasive shrubs rapidly took over the ungrazed hills, turning them into scrublands. Since the formation of the Conservation Volunteers in the late 1950s, areas of this have been cleared but, without grazing, this is a recurring task.

There has been a certain amount of movement back to sheep in recent years which, together with the recovery of rabbit numbers, should ease the losses in limited areas. Interesting results have been obtained by the National Trust too, who have grazed sheep on a number of their downland properties, including Box Hill and Ranmore.

Much grazing for conservation purposes has been limited to the winter, when the sheep will not eat the flowers which it is intended to protect. However, in some cases, the grass which has developed during the absence of grazing comprises coarse species like tor grass, which need heavy grazing to eliminate. For this reason, summer grazing is also practised on a rotational basis.

Apart from grazing, other methods have been tried. Mowing and burning both have the disadvantage of increasing the nutrient status of the soil, which may exacerbate the problem in the long term. Burning has the added disadvantage of killing off large numbers of invertebrates.

Except where woodland exists, or where scrub has invaded, much of the North Downs grassland has survived between the Kent border and Guildford. Beyond Guildford, construction of the main road to Farnham has combined with agriculture to destroy much of the interesting flora of the Hog's Back. The main survivor along this stretch is the SWT reserve of Seale Chalk Pit.

Grasses are clearly a major component of the downland flora. A number of species are present and occur in a variety of combinations. The finer species allow a more varied flora to develop, whilst certain others may be dominant, supressing other plants.

Of the dominant species, upright brome can be said to be far too common in the county. Tor grass also dominates considerable areas.

The commonest finer grasses are common quaking grass, meadow oat grass, downy oat grass, crested hair grass and smaller cat's tail. Other species, like red fescue, sheep's fescue and crested dog's tail, are common throughout the county.

Some grasses are rather restricted in their distribution. The mat grass fescue is known from only one site in the Chipstead Valley, although it is found on a number of chalk sites in Kent. Fern grass, however, needs land where it is free from competition.

Two sedges are also important components of chalk grassland. Glaucous sedge is common throughout the county, whilst spring sedge is frequent on a range of habitats.

Of all the chalk downland plants, the best known are perhaps the orchids. Surrey has a wide variety of species, some of which are quite common, others rather rare. Numbers of individuals within a species vary widely from year to year, largely due to their complex life cycles. Many species take several years to reach maturity and flower, and then do not flower every year.

As its name suggests, one of the commonest downland orchids is the common spotted. Apart from the chalk, it is also to be found on other base rich grasslands. Confined to the chalk, but often growing with common spotted orchids, is the much rarer fragrant orchid. Where it occurs it is often plentiful, yet it is only a tenth as widespread as the common spotted. The pyramidal orchid, found in roughly the same areas as the fragrant, has a much more compact pink flower. It has been reported off the chalk in the Godalming area, and grows, along with many other chalkland plants, on a section of Witley Common, where chalk was once brought in to construct tracks for the military.

The elaborate flower of the bee orchid is designed to fool bees into thinking it is one of their own kind visiting a flower. If they try to mate with it, some of the pollen is brushed off onto their bodies, thus aiding pollination when the bee lands on the next orchid. Its main habitat is chalk grassland, but it can also be found on some clays and gravels. Like other plants, bee orchids are not averse to growing in areas where they may not be expected, were it not for the activities of Man. A group found in 1974 near a broken-down wall on the acid soils of Hankley Common were undoubtedly taking advantage of the lime in the mortar, whereas those that grow on the Thameside Ham Lands near Richmond thrive on imported soil used to fill old gravel workings.

The much smaller fly orchid is a little less common and certainly harder to find. Growing in grass along wood edges, scrub and disused quarries, it is difficult to spot among the coarser grasses and varies in number considerably from year to year.

Whilst the twayblade may be ubiquitous in many parts of Surrey, other orchids of grasslands are particularly rare. Among the chalk species, marsh helleborine is perhaps one of the rarest, having been found in 1963 on Box Hill, after a break of one hundred years. Since then, it has been recorded from the same site on a number of occasions.

Box Hill has also been a location for the erratic lizard orchid over the years, as have several other sites. Most of these records were during the early part of the twentieth century. Today, there are

ABOVE LEFT: Common poppy. RIGHT: Box. BELOW LEFT: Fragrant orchid; CENTRE: bee and musk orchids and RIGHT: Common spotted orchid.

PLATE I

LEFT: Primrose; ABOVE: toothwort and CENTRE: bird's-nest orchid.
BELOW LEFT: Wood sorrel and RIGHT: common frog.

PLATE II

occasional reports of this species. It has been suggested that some past records could be due to seed carried by high-level air currents from France, where it is far more common.

Autumn lady's tresses, another rare orchid, is known from about twenty localities in Surrey, including the southern slopes of Box Hill. Musk orchids, which are extremely tiny, are found on the Zig Zag slopes of the same site, as well as the Hackhurst Down and White Down area near Abinger Hammer. At Headley Warren reserve, near Leatherhead, long-term studies of musk orchid populations are carried out. The frog orchid is also limited to a few localities, the most frequent records being from Merrow Downs near Guildford.

Of the remaining orchids, the greater butterfly may be found in small and decreasing numbers in grassland and more wooded habitats in a number of locations. From time to time there are more spectacular displays of this plant, as happened early in the 1980s at Sheepleas. Where it occurs, the man orchid may also be found in similar habitats, often in large colonies.

Although perhaps the best known of the chalk plants, the orchids are far from being the only flowers of interest. A wide range of species provide colour throughout the growing season, many adding to the pleasure of a downland walk by their scent. Among the commonest species in Surrey are marjoram, lady's bedstraw, common birdsfoot trefoil and field scabious. Other less common, but widespread species include small scabious, kidney vetch, horseshoe vetch and common rockrose. Dropwort replaces the larger meadowsweet on the Downs.

Both large thyme and wild thyme are local in Surrey, the former being the most common. Basil thyme is similarly distributed and virtually confined to chalk. It has, however, been found elsewhere, where chalk soil has been introduced.

Gentians are a feature of chalk downland, although the early gentian is rare in Surrey. Regular sites appear to be Banstead Downs and Riddlesdown. Felwort, or autumn gentian, is far more widespread. It is locally common in the county.

Common spotted orchid

Some of the chalk plants, whilst growing in the general grassland environment, cannot stand any competition from other species. As a result, they grow only on bare chalk, where the surface has been broken. The rarest of these, cut-leaved germander is confined to few sites, one of which is the chalk slopes of Fames Rough near Chipstead Valley. At the same site, a slightly commoner species, ground pine, may also be found. This small, yellow-flowered plant looks rather like a tiny pine, but is actually related to bugle, a common plant throughout the county. Where cut-leaved germander and ground pine are known to grow, delicate conservation work can aid their survival. Elsewhere, they may appear where viable seeds remain in the soil, if this is subsequently disturbed by Man, or burrowing animals like rabbits.

Another plant of disturbed chalk soil is candytuft. Whilst it may also occur as a casual escape from gardens, the wild plant is only reported from the Box Hill area. In one locality it reappeared after a considerable number of years following tree clearance, then maintained a population which fluctuated from year to year.

In May and June milkworts add a sprinkling of blue, pink and white to the Downs. Variable in colour, both the common milkwort and chalk milkwort may be seen. Common milkwort is also found on grassland off the chalk.

Before the milkworts, in March and April, hairy violets dot the hillside. With deep mauve flowers, hairy violet is closely associated with chalk grassland.

At one time, the fading of the violets heralded the bright yellow of the cowslip. Now, although still found in many areas, cowslips have declined. Partly this is due to the ploughing of its old haunts or the invasion of scrub. However, pressure from picking has had a major influence on numbers, especially in the north of Surrey, nearest London. It was in only 1827 that cowslips were recorded as near to central London as Stockwell.

Two plants of the chalk grassland, which are generally a little taller than the average sward, are yellow-wort and common centaury. The former is common along the Downs, and may be identified by its small yellow flowers and unusual leaves. The leaves come in opposite pairs on the stem, and are joined together at the base. This gives the impression of the stalk having pierced the stem. The latter has pink flowers and is found in a range of other habitats including heathland and woodland rides. The related lesser centaury is far rarer. It likes damp places, such as old pastures, but may also be seen on the chalk.

A common plant, flowering between July and September, is the harebell. An attractive, short, blue-flowered plant, it is found on both alkaline and acid grasslands, but is absent from the clay soils. A related plant, the clustered bellflower, is locally common in the county. Commonest on chalk grassland, it also grows on alluvial meadows near the Thames.

Another *Campanula*, the round-headed rampion, is found in a number of localities in Surrey. The plant itself is confined to southern England, also growing in Sussex, Hampshire and Wiltshire. An important site for this species is Hackhurst Downs, where regular scrub clearance aims to maintain reasonable populations.

Eyebright is a small, common plant of grasslands throughout the county. The flowers are typically white, or tinged with purple, and appear between June and September. Much work has been done by Surrey botanists in the past, resulting in the naming of several species, many of which are infertile. An interesting aspect of this plant is that it is semi-parasitic on other species.

Yellow rattle is another semi-parasitic plant, particularly of grasses. Flowering from May to September, it is uncommon in Surrey and seems to have declined over the past fifty years. Closely related, but considerably rarer, is the greater yellow rattle. First identified in the county in the 1960s, it seems to be largely confined to the Chipstead area. Although larger than the yellow rattle, it is extremely difficult to identify. Yet another semi-parasite, bastard toadflax, obtains some of its nutrients from the roots of downland herbs. This is a plant of short turf, especially where it has been grazed. Rare, it is restricted to the Downs between Pewley and Purley.

Some plants are totally parasitic. In particular, the broomrapes must be mentioned. Attached to the roots of their hosts from which they obtain nourishment, these brownish coloured plants are variable in number and locality. Knapweed broomrape is parasitic on the greater knapweed, a plant locally common on the chalk. Common broomrape, whilst occurring mainly on the chalk, can be found in other areas too. It is parasitic on any plants, especially clovers.

Although rabbits are common on the Downs, and do a considerable amount of useful grazing, they do find some plants unpalatable. Species like nettle and elder do particularly well around warrens, no doubt helped by the rabbit droppings. Other plants taking advantage of such situations are hound's tongue, viper's bugloss and many thistles.

The mauves, pinks and reds of thistles are a common sight on the Downs. A species which is particularly noticeable to picnickers is the locally abundant dwarf thistle. It thrives on areas which are regularly grazed or trampled, as it is able to prevent leaf damage by pressing itself hard against the ground. Carline thistle is largely confined to the chalk, where it may be common. Less frequent is the musk thistle, whilst the woolly thistle is decidedly rare. Most records for this species come from the Caterham area and relate to just a few plants. As thistles look rather alike to many people, populations of such rare species are under threat from unintentional destruction during tidying-up operations.

Rabbits also take advantage of the numerous hills of the yellow meadow ant. By sitting on top, the rabbit obtains a far clearer view of the surrounding area. The droppings deposited by the animals often lead to luxuriant growth of vegetation on these hills, especially plants like thyme and marjoram. Periodically, yellow meadow ant hills are destroyed, as green woodpeckers are rather partial to their occupants.

Invertebrates play an important part in the ecology of the Surrey chalklands. In particular, butterflies are a speciality. Perhaps most characteristic are the blues.

Most places will support the common blue in summer. Lesser numbers of other related species may also be seen, including the Adonis, chalkhill and small blues. In the mid-1970s, both the Adonis and small blue were declining and thought to be in danger of disappearing from Surrey. Since then, the Adonis blue has increased in the county and spread westwards. A colony of the small blue at Pewley Down near Guildford has remained strong. The same locality is also home to the other species.

A group of small butterflies, the skippers, are characteristic of Surrey grasslands. One species of this rather moth-like group, the silver spotted skipper, is confined in England to the chalk hills of the south. In Surrey, it has lost much ground over recent decades, and is now nationally endangered. It needs short turf on steep slopes to breed, conditions which are now mainly found between Box Hill and Buckland. The main cause of the decline of this and other species has probably been the scrubbing over of grassland due to lack of grazing. Yet mowing to prevent this has also contributed, by being carried out at the wrong time of year.

Among the commonest grassland butterflies are the meadow brown and gatekeeper. The marbled white (also a member of the brown family) is frequent on the Downs, especially in areas of longer grass. A much more local butterfly, the Duke of Burgundy fritillary, is mainly an insect of woodland clearings. However, its larval foodplant is cowslip, which necessitates it venturing into grasslands.

A wide range of moths may be seen flying over the chalk hills. Among the most familiar are the five-spot and six-spot burnets. Both species feed on bird's-foot-trefoil, a range of clovers and similar plants, during the caterpillar stage. Some five-spot burnet moths can take two years to progress from egg to maturity. The burnet companion and Mother Shipton moth also feed on these plants. They may often be seen in company with burnet moths. The Mother Shipton, which flies in May and June, overwinters as a chrysalis.

Wild clematis, which scrambles over trees around the edge of most chalk grassland, is food to caterpillars of a number of species, among them the small emerald, small waved umber and pretty chalk carpet. Haworth's pug, which flies in July and August, feeds on the flower buds of wild clematis. The fern moth, flying a month or so earlier, also feeds on buttercups.

Common mouse ear, a plant regularly found on the Downs, is food to the caterpillar of the small yellow underwing moth. This species has a green caterpillar, with one central dark green, and two whitish lines, along its back. It feeds on the flowers and seeds of the plant, boring into unripe capsules to reach the seeds if necessary.

Among other typical species are the lace border (a distinctively marked white moth), common carpet, shaded broad bar and the chalk carpet. A small, brightly metallic moth which frequently visits large, showy flowers like ox-eye daisies, is *Micropteryx calthella*. Its larvae feed on mosses.

Small moths are just one aspect of the fauna of chalk grassland, which is the province of specialists. At Headley Warren reserve, the main field is known as Stainton's Field, in memory of a well-known 19th century lepidopterist, who specialised in this group.

A number of other groups of insects are well represented both at Headley Warren and other grassland sites in the county. Box Hill is among the top places in Britain for insects, although this could be due to more people having studied them there, than elsewhere. However, more information is undoubtedly needed on groups such as millipedes, centipedes, woodlice and mites, from all grassland localities.

One of the most famous Surrey insects is a beetle – the glow-worm. The name derives from the female which, whilst not looking like a worm, does not look like a beetle either. The male is far more beetle-like in appearance. The insects give out light at all stages of their life, from egg onwards. However, it is the adult female which emits the strongest light.

The light is produced by luciferin, a substance which reacts with oxygen and water. The light is pale greenish-blue, and is a particularly impressive sight when many females are together. It is designed to attract the males, and can be shut off when not required. This is probably done by reducing the amount of oxygen reaching luciferin in the last three abdominal segments of the body, from which the light is emitted. The adults are thought to feed little, if at all, but the larva is a predator of small slugs and snails. It injects a substance into the prey from its jaws, which serves to reduce the prey to liquid. The reliance of glow worm larvae on snails restricts them to the chalk. It is only here that snails can obtain the calcium needed to form their shells.

As may be supposed, snails are common on the chalk grasslands. One rather impressive species is the Roman snail. This is the largest European species, with a shell diameter of up to 50mm. It is rather common on the North Downs and is the species which features frequently on Continental menus. It may be seen in a number of localities, including the Headley Warren reserve. It prefers tall herbage.

Downland abounds with many other species, among the most attractive of which are the banded snails. These belong to the same family as the Roman snail, but are only half its size. They come in a range of colours and patterns, all distinctively marked. Two species are present, the white-lipped banded snail and the dark-lipped. As the names suggest, the colour of the lip of the shell is the main identifying characteristic, although this is an unreliable feature. A rare Mediterranean snail, *Trochoidea elegans*, has occasionally been recorded on dry grassland in south-east England, so may well be worth looking out for.

In summer the 'song' of grasshoppers and crickets emanates from the grass. Many members of this group are insects of the tropics, but around thirty are found in Britain. Each species has a different 'song' which is produced not by the mouth, but by rubbing two parts of the body together. In the grasshoppers, this involves rubbing a series of pegs on the leg against the wing. Crickets have their pegs on the wings, so rub two wings together. Movements of the grasshopper leg can be at a rate of up to twenty times per second.

All species eat grass and, except for the meadow grasshopper, all Surrey species can fly. The county fauna includes the common field and common green grasshoppers, the stripe-winged grasshopper (which has a white stripe on the wing) and the rufous grasshopper which has white-tipped antennae.

In July and August, wild parsnip is a common plant in Surrey grasslands, particularly on the chalk. Its flowers are attractive to a wide range of insects, including large numbers of soldier beetles. These matt red beetles have elongated bodies which are rather soft. Their colour indicates to potential predators their distastefulness. As they are carnivorous creatures they presumably visit the flowers to launch attacks on other insects, but may frequently be seen mating. A disproportionate number of soldier beetles are found mating compared to other insects. This is thought to be due to the excessive time this species takes over the activity.

Not only soldier beetles visit the wild parsnip. It is the place to observe a whole host of creatures, including a wasp-like fly, *Conops quadrifasciatus*. This insect parasitises bumble bees, actively chasing them to lay an egg on their body whilst in flight. Other flies also take advantage of wild parsnip to launch attacks. In particular, the bristly dance fly may be seen leaping onto neighbouring insects.

A typical piece of Surrey downland probably supports some 250 species of spider. Of these, wolf spiders such as *Pardosa monticola*, are frequently seen running over the surface. They have no webs, but actively pursue their prey through the short grass. The females may often be seen carrying their egg sacs beneath their bodies. Once the young have hatched, they are carried around on the back of their mother.

Near the ground, often on the sunny side of meadow ant hills, may be found the silk tubes of *Atypus affinis*, a species of trap-door spider. The spider excavates a deep hole in the ground. This is lined with silk, which is continued to form a silk tube above the surface. The exposed tube is then covered with soil, making it difficult to spot. When any potential prey walks over it, the spider rushes up the tube, attacking it with its fangs.

In practice, acid grasslands are associated with heathlands. Whilst pure stands of acid grassland do occur, they are often so tied up with heathland that plants such as ling and gorse may be found too. In some areas, however, acid grassland is doing well. Fires in 1976, for instance, enabled the clearance of light woodland from parts of Headley Heath, so allowing the re-establishment of grassland cover. Other patches may be found along wide forestry rides.

On wetter areas, this habitat may be dominated by purple moor grass. Drier conditions allow the development of other species like heath grass, wavy hair grass, early hair grass and silver hair grass. Typically encountered with such grasses are flowers like tormentil, creeping cinquefoil, heath bedstraw and harebell. Some sedges are also typical of this habitat, including *Carex binervis* (most common in the west of Surrey) and *Carex pilulifera*. Plants like black medick grow equally well on chalk or acid grassland.

Neutral grassland, where the soil is neither acid nor alkaline, is now a great rarity in Surrey, as elsewhere. Modern agriculture has either ploughed or fertilised almost every meadow in the county, increasing agricultural production at the expense of wildflowers. In the past, such meadows were used by farmers for rough grazing or hay production.

Some types of meadowland were flooded regularly in winter. This was either because they were low-lying and so inundated with water at times of heavy rain, or because they were deliberately flooded by the use of artificial channels. Whilst flooding may at first seem to reduce their suitability for grazing, it was actually beneficial. The constant movement of flowing water prevented grasses being delayed by frosts, so enabling spring grazing to commence some three to four weeks earlier. The management of the ditches used to flood these meadows was a labour-intensive task, so is now uneconomic. Other meadows, where the water table was close to the surface or where there are natural springs, were simply wet. Today, most of these wet areas have been drained.

In neighbouring counties like Berkshire, a beautiful indicator of old, unploughed meadows is the fritillary. Surrey is not thought to support any of these plants in the wild, although they grew in Thameside meadows between Mortlake and Kew until 1876. A few fritillaries are established, however, on private land in places, probably as remnants of old gardens. A dozen or so appear each year in a small piece of grassland near Dorking, for instance.

Several species of orchid may be encountered on acid or neutral soils. The common spotted orchid appears in a number of localities, as does the twayblade. On places like Epsom Common, the southern marsh orchid can be a spectacular feature, with exceptionally long flower spikes being frequent. Early purple orchids and green winged orchids have both experienced a spectacular decline in recent decades, largely due to the ploughing of old meadows.

Damp conditions, particularly on clay or chalk, provide an excellent chance to see one of our most unusual ferns. The adder's-tongue has a short stem, with a single oval leaf and single flower spike, looking rather like a greater plantain. Found in grassy places throughout the county, it is most irregular in appearance. Between November and April it dies away, leaving no evidence above ground.

A wide range of grasses may be found on the clay and alluvium soils. Crested dog's tail and yellow oatgrass prefer dry conditions. Meadow barley grows on both Thameside alluvium and clay, whilst meadow foxtail especially prefers alluvium. Perennial ryegrass is well suited to withstand trampling. Common species include timothy, red fescue, sheep's fescue, soft brome and Yorkshire fog. The first of this group may be native in a few places, but is also an important agricultural grass.

Several grasslands may support a range of relatively robust, colourful species like dandelion, meadow buttercup, bulbous buttercup, ox-eye daisy, common sorrel and various clovers. These even survive where horses graze, but vanish if grazing is intense.

In 1981, the Surrey Wildlife Trust took the opportunity to acquire a reserve near Elstead, known as Thundry Meadows. The reserve includes several botanically rich meadows and some ordinary agricultural grassland, alongside the River Wey. To keep the botanical diversity, it is necessary for a limited amount of grazing to take place. In order to achieve this at the correct time of year, the Trust decided to purchase their own small beef herd.

In the wet meadows on the reserve plants like large bitter cress, marsh marigold, ragged robin, yellow iris, marsh violet and marsh cinquefoil grow. Two species of sweet grass grow, *Glyceria fluitans* and *Glyceria plicata*. In the dry meadows climbing corydalis is abundant, scrambling over the large grass tussocks. Dyer's greenweed is also well represented here.

Near Epsom, Horton Country Park has been established on an area of old agricultural land previously owned by the many hospitals in the area. A section of about 50 acres is maintained as a hay meadow and developing an interesting flora. No fertilizers are used, but the vegetation is cut annually to prevent woody and coarse species gaining dominance.

Perhaps the most important neutral grassland in Surrey is Staines Moor near Heathrow Airport. Although at present safe, it is under regular threat from companies wishing to dig it up for gravel. The Moor is an area of about 100 hectares of ancient alluvial grassland mentioned in the Domesday Book. It was then part of a larger area of common land used for the grazing of cattle, horses and geese. It appears to have been maintained in this way ever since, there being no record of it having been ploughed.

The geological and hydrological diversity at Staines has led to a site which is unique in southeast England. Well over 300 different plants and 130 birds have been recorded, which indicates an equally rich diversity of insects.

Although grasslands are clearly most important for their botanical and entomological species, there are also a limited number of specialist birds.

Among the most typical of these is the skylark, a bird which is noticeable more in flight than when at rest. Nesting on the ground, often in areas without trees, it must sing in flight to proclaim its territory. Although not the commonest, the skylark is probably the most widely distributed bird in Britain. Another 'in flight' singer, the meadow pipit, makes its voice heard as it parachutes earthwards. This insect eater is a major victim of the cuckoo, which regularly replaces one meadow pipit egg for one of its own. The more local tree pipit needs areas of grassland, interspersed with a few trees, from which it sings.

The yellowhammer with a distinctive song, said to sound like a 'little bit of bread and no cheese', feeds on weed seeds, wild fruits and various invertebrates. It nests in clumps of grass, bramble, bracken and other low vegetation. The nest is well concealed, as is that of the reed bunting and woodlark. Both these species use long grass, thistles and other plants, as convenient song posts.

A bird with a high-pitched reeling call and found on grassy commons, is the grasshopper warbler. This species often nests in the dense, tangled vegetation found around the edge of the grassland. It frequently sings in drizzling, overcast weather, around dawn or dusk.

Among the larger birds are lapwings, which have a widespread, if thin distribution across Surrey. Among their favourite sites are damp and wet meadows along the valleys of the Wey and Mole.

Small mammals form the prey of birds such as kestrel, frequently seen hunting over grasslands. Typical mammals of these areas in Surrey are short-tailed (or field) vole, common shrew and pygmy shrew. Field mice may also be found, especially where short-tailed voles are rare or absent.

Hobby (TP)

Although formerly a woodland animal, moles are now common in meadows and pastures. Usually molehills are the only obvious sign of their presence. Their distribution indicates them to be tolerant of waterlogged soils. Fresh molehills may even be seen in deep frozen soil.

Bookham Common grasslands are of particular significance because of long-term studies made by the London Natural History Society. Over the years, there have been considerable changes at this site. Before 1914, the grassy plains were grazed by cattle and sheep. This decreased until, by 1949, all grazing had ceased. The grass became tussocky. This had many effects on the wildlife of the area, not least changes to bird species. Snipe ceased breeding in the 1920s, stonechat and whinchat in the 1930s, and linnet, skylark and tree pipit since. Changes at Bookham continue today. Scrub is constantly invading the grassland, which is then cleared, to restore open areas.

This is typical of all grassland. Without grazing or scrub clearance, grassland is in constant danger of being lost. Its conservation is especially important in Surrey, where the warmer climate allows species limited in their distribution to retain a foothold.

ABOVE: Chalk grass meadow, Ranmore. (KB) BELOW: Chalk grassland, Box Hill. (KB).

ABOVE: A yew tree casts a dense shadow on a chalk meadow. (KB) BELOW: Damp meadow at Thundry Meadows reserve, with a range of grasses, sedges and rushes. (KB)

ABOVE: With the exception of thistles, closely grazed grassland can only support ground-hugging plants. (KB) BELOW: Rough grassland at Thundry Meadows – favourite haunt of many butterfly species. (KB)

42

ABOVE: Open parkland near Betchworth, ideal for hole-nesting species such as kestrel and little owl. (KB) BELOW: Rough village common, rich in wildflowers and butterflies.

LEFT: Early purple orchid. (RST) ABOVE: Adder's tongue fern. CENTRE: Common rockrose on chalk grassland. BELOW: Greater butterfly orchid.

44

LEFT: Thorpe (hay) Meadow. (RS) RIGHT: Grasshopper (meadow).
(DAE) BELOW: Yellow meadow anthill on chalk grassland.

45

ABOVE: Gorse and heather on Thursley Common. (KB) BELOW:
Purple moor grass on heathland. INSET: Silver-studded blue on
Thursley Common. (DAE)

46

Heathlands

Until Mesolithic Man arrived in the county around ten thousand years ago, the Surrey heaths were a mixture of oak and hazel woodland. This woodland would have been lighter than that which grew on the clay, due to poorer soils, but trees, rather than heather, were certainly the dominant vegetation.

Mesolithic Man seems to have preferred the sandy heathlands of west Surrey to any other part of the county. The light woodland cover was particularly suited to his food-gathering activities and nomadic way of life.

As the Neolithic period dawned, a gradual transformation to a more settled agriculture took place. In the early stages, slash-and-burn methods would have provided rough grazing for stock on the heathlands. As the Bronze and Iron Age cultures developed, so did agriculture. More permanent stock-raising became important.

Grazing continued on the heathlands until, in most cases, the twentieth century. At Thursley Common, for example, grazing ended in 1922. During the 18th and 19th centuries, pressure from animal husbandry was particularly great, most heaths probably being almost treeless at this time.

Heathland is, therefore, a totally artificial habitat in Surrey, which only developed due to the interference of Man. Natural heathlands occur only on the coasts in this country. The southern lowland heaths are distinct from the moors found in northern and western Britain in several ways.

Although heathland of a similar type is found in a number of European countries from Spain and France to Norway and Sweden, the habitat in Britain is largely confined to Surrey, Sussex, Suffolk, Hampshire, Dorset and Cornwall. Two of the largest tracts survive in Surrey. In the Chobham area, heathland covers some 2,000 hectares, whilst south of the Hog's Back, Thursley, Hankley and Frensham Commons add another 1,400 hectares.

Heathland has primarily developed on sandy soils following grazing. These soils are well drained, enabling nutrients to be quickly washed from the upper layers. The absence of trees prevents such nutrients being returned to the surface, so a leached soil develops. The acid conditions are favoured by plants such as heathers.

In Surrey, the majority of heathlands are found on the various Greensand soils. These include all those in the south-west of the county around Thursley, Frensham and Hindhead, and others in the Leith Hill area. In north-west Surrey, the Chobham group of heaths lies on the Bagshot Beds. Patches of marine gravel high on the Downs give rise to the isolated heathlands around Headley and Walton-on-the-Hill.

47

The most typical plants of heathland are, of course, the heathers. These principally comprise ling, bell heather, and cross-leaved heath. Ling dominates the dry heath areas in most places, with bell heather locally common. Cross-leaved heath prefers damper conditions.

In many places, cessation of grazing and subsequent disturbances of the soils have led to the invasion of birch, pine and bracken at the expense of the heathers.

Headley Heath, and the more isolated heaths of the North Downs, suffer little from pine invasion. Here, silver birch is a problem. Once, Headley Heath was grazed by sheep from Betchworth, Brockham and Headley, under the charge of a common shepherd. During the Second World War, military training destroyed much of the vegetation. Birch, being quick to invade, took advantage of the bare soil, soon covering extensive areas.

Subsequent accidental fires have made substantial inroads into parts of the birch cover. The National Trust has taken the opportunity to keep these areas open, thereby aiding the recolonisation of heather.

Whilst fires have been advantageous in the clearance of woodland from some heaths, they have also tended to encourage the spread of bracken.

After a bad fire, heathers must regenerate from seed, whereas the deep rhizomes of bracken survive relatively unscathed. Consequently, they are often able to regrow within weeks of being burned, thereby taking over former heather areas.

Once established, bracken is extremely difficult to eradicate. Various methods may be used, one of which involves digging up the total rhizome network. As this can reach a considerable depth, it is impractical. However, at Headley Heath, turf removed by Kew Gardens from a bracken area has allowed it to be successfully resown with heather.

Other methods of bracken control include the regular mowing of the plant, and spraying areas with Asulox. Mowing, especially if regularly carried out before the fronds unfurl, weakens the plant, so it eventually dies. Asulox is a chemical which is specific to bracken. It appears to be effective for several years.

Bracken does support some forms of associated wildlife, but the number of species is small. A number of moth caterpillars use it as a foodplant. These include the brown moth, small angle shades, brown silver line and orange swift. Caterpillars of the map-winged swift and gold swift moths, feed on bracken roots.

Overlying the chalk, the marine gravel heath at Headley exhibits a particularly interesting feature. Part of Headley Heath is acid heathland whilst another valley is chalk grassland. At the boundary of these two geological formations, a vegetation called chalk heath has developed. Here, on the mixed soils, heather and gorse grow alongside bee orchid and yellow-wort.

Away from the hilltop heaths of the Downs, the rest of Surrey heathland suffers from the invasion of Scots pine. This is frequently due to seeding from plantations growing on adjacent areas, whose boundaries gradually move forward across the heath if left unchecked. Rapid growth and large numbers of seeds necessitates vigorous control. Generally, this involves either pulling up young pines, or cutting down older ones.

The age and vigour of the various heather species largely depends on the frequency and intensity of fires. Little controlled burning, as practised in Scotland, takes place on the Surrey heaths. Most fires are either accidental, or the result of vandalism, so burn the heathers indiscriminately.

As ling grows from the centre outwards, the inner part eventually dies, to leave a ring of growth indicative of older plants. Because of fires in 1976, only around 20% of the ling has reached this stage at Thursley, it having developed after previous extensive burning in the 1950s. The remainder of the common comprises younger plants, heading towards maturity.

On the dry heath, ling and bell heather are usually interspersed with gorse. In places, dwarf gorse and petty whin occur too. These last two species are very much oceanic plants, preferring the more humid conditions here, to the drier ones of continental Europe.

48

ABOVE: Moat pond, Thursley. BELOW: Thursley Bog.

PLATE III

ABOVE: Dead wood amid heather several years after a fire. BELOW:
Heathland being invaded by pine.

PLATE IV

Some patches of gorse are extensive, particularly where heather has become degenerate. Apart from being attractive, with yellow flowers throughout the year, they also support an interesting parasitic plant, dodder. This grows on both ling and gorse, and is locally abundant in this habitat.

Also of interest in the areas of gorse, particularly at Thursley, is the rare Dartford warbler. At the northern extent of its breeding range, this resident, long-tailed, insectivorous bird is subject to considerable fluctuations in numbers. Weather is the main cause of this, severe cold having disastrous consequences.

After numbers had built up during the 1950s, cold weather during the winters of 1961/2 and 1962/3 wiped out the population. Evidence of breeding next came in 1969, north of the Hog's Back. Once again numbers grew, until the fires of 1976. However, a population was maintained, growing, at least on Thursley, through to 1984. Then, there were twenty pairs on the common. More cold weather at the start of 1985 reduced numbers to fifteen pairs which survived, despite the dismal and cold summer. The extreme prolonged cold of the 1985/6 winter though, is likely to herald a further decline.

A regular summer visitor to Surrey is the nightjar, a nocturnal, insect-eating bird, preying on moths, beetles and other flying insects. Also found in young plantations, it is a secretive bird, best known for its churring call, which usually commences some time after sunset. In 1909, it was still recorded in Dulwich and Streatham, but has since vanished from all localities close to London, even as far out as Headley Heath. Chobham Common and the west Surrey heaths are now its stronghold, as well as the heathy areas around Leith Hill. The general decline of this species has been due to a combination of urban encroachment, the maturing of conifer plantations, and disturbance. It is a ground-nesting bird, so dogs must take much of the blame in places like Headley Heath and Horsell Common.

For all heathland species, fragmentation of suitable habitat is a serious threat to survival. Without a large enough area in which to breed and feed, populations are liable to fall below a size which remains viable.

Fragmentation can arise from a variety of causes. Building developments, road construction and other uses can reduce the extent of heathlands, whilst fires can change the structure of the vegetation. Often rare species such as the Dartford warbler and woodlark require such different habitats as to increase and decrease at the expense of each other.

Old ling, around 25 or more years of age, is ideal for Dartford warblers and other species such as stonechat. However, woodlarks are declining, as their preference is for ling under 25cm high. This becomes a liability as the ling ages.

Where drainage becomes impeded, wet heath develops. Cross-leaved heath then increases considerably, and a range of other characteristic species are found. Among these are the insectivorous common sundew and long-leaved sundew. In western Surrey, the rare marsh clubmoss also grows, largely on bare, black peaty soil, by tracks.

An even rarer plant, the brown beak sedge, grows at Thursley. It has been recorded for well over fifty years, but has varied in quantity and precise location over this period. Like marsh clubmoss, it prefers moist, bare peat, where it has no competition with other vegetation.

Dominant in many places, and found throughout the wet heathland, is purple moor grass. Although occurring in localities throughout the county, this plant is especially associated with the west Surrey heaths. Some people are of the opinion that it is indicative of the drier wet heaths and that it is spreading in places.

Wet heath is basically a transitional habitat, usually present between areas of dry heath and bog. Consequently, a variety of plants from both these habitats may be present. Drier areas often support small clumps of ling, whereas various sphagnum mosses, cotton grass, bog asphodel, cranberry and several rushes grow in the damper flushes.

In certain conditions bog may develop where drainage is impeded. Different plant communities exist in these permanently waterlogged conditions, although these vary somewhat, depending on water levels and acidity. The depth of peat deposits can also have a bearing on the plants present, as can the amount of competition with other species.

Apart from being dangerous to walk on, bog vegetation is also particularly susceptible to trampling. The Thursley, Ockham and Bagmoor bog is probably the finest in south-east England, but not the only one in Surrey. Bogs also occur on the Bagshot Beds, especially at West End Common, Bisley Common, Lightwater Bog and Colony Bog. Many of these sites are used for military training, so are inaccessible to the general public.

The bog areas support some birds otherwise not found breeding in Surrey. Curlew regularly breed at Thursley, this probably being the last site in the county. Redshank, which have bred irregularly in Surrey, also once frequented Thursley, but have long since disappeared. Not necessarily confined to wet heathland, but regularly breeding there, is the snipe.

The bogs at Thursley are varied in nature, and have been studied in some detail. They provide a good indication of what may be found elsewhere, and are relatively easily accessible. In total, five distinct bogs have been recognised.

The east bog is largely maintained by percolating groundwater. Sphagnum mosses are particularly characteristic, with eight species occurring. The commonest, *Sphagnum papillosum*, covers 70% of the bog, forming frequent hummocks. *Sphagnum pulchum* covers about a fifth of the area, with other species making up the remainder. Part of the bog exhibits plants indicative of slightly drier conditions, such as purple moor grass, ling and cross-leaved heath. Although described as a valley bog, the absence of sedges and reeds is more characteristic of a raised bog. The rare Hare's-tail cottongrass (as opposed to common cottongrass) grows here. Elsewhere, it is found in the Bisley, Chobham, Frensham and Leith Hill areas.

Completely different in nature is Pudmore bog. Here, common cottongrass grows, together with greater tussock sedge, the more local bottle sedge, and common reed. Other plants include bog hair grass, marsh cinquefoil, bog asphodel, both sundews, white beaked sedge and brown beak sedge.

Middle bog has certain similarities with Pudmore bog as it partly shares the same water source. It contains both Royal fern and large colonies of bog asphodel.

The water supplying Western bog is less acid and faster-moving than that serving the other bogs. Consequently, the flora is totally different and includes reedmace, meadow thistle, early marsh orchid, bog pimpernel, lesser skullcap, carnation sedge, soft rush, sharp flowered rush, jointed rush, bulbous rush and black bog rush. Several species of Sphagnum may be found, including three uncommon ones, *Sphagnum fibriatum, S. palustre* and *S. squarosum*. The influence of stream water acidity on a bog is well illustrated here, as a marked change to species more characteristic of acid bog conditions occurs only a short distance away from the flowing water.

South bog has many similarities with Western bog, but is particularly important for Royal fern and marsh clubmoss. There is also an area of wet willow and birch woodland.

Whether wet or dry, the flora of heathland is rather restricted in variety. This applies equally to the larger vertebrates, although several of these are of special interest.

Perhaps the best known are the birds. Apart from the Dartford warbler, stonechat, woodlark and nightjar, other specialist breeders are to be found. These include the hobby, a rare, migratory bird of prey, which needs large areas over which to hunt. Heathlands are especially important in this respect, as they provide open areas largely devoid of trees for hunting, with the occasional clump to permit nesting.

Other birds of prey use heathland for breeding, including sparrowhawks and kestrels, but these are not restricted to this habitat. Owls also hunt on the heaths, especially tawny and little owls.

More regular breeding birds include the yellowhammer, redpoll and linnet. Whilst distributed over a range of habitats, all three species are commonly encountered on Surrey heaths. Often, they reach their highest breeding density in this habitat.

Winter provides the chance of seeing a range of other hunting birds, including merlin, hen harrier and great grey shrike. As small mammals are comparatively scarce on heathlands, such birds largely feed on other birds.

Mammals, such as stoats, weasels and hedgehogs are rather uncommon on heaths, but foxes range widely. Sometimes foxes and badgers may be found breeding, but more often they just use the heath for hunting. Deer are also quite frequent, especially roe deer, which are widespread in Surrey. Other species have been reported in the past, and muntjac are seen from time to time. Rabbits are found in this habitat, which is also one of the areas where hares, generally uncommon in Surrey, may be seen.

Bats have been little studied anywhere until recent years, so little is known of their distribution. A bat group, formed in Surrey during 1985, hopes to rectify this, but until then we must rely on incomplete records, largely based on casual sightings. Once again, taking Thursley as an example, whiskered, Daubenton's, Leisler's, noctule and brown long-eared bat have been recorded, in addition to the tiny pipistrelle.

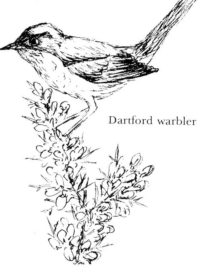

Dartford warbler

Of particular interest among the vertebrates are the reptiles and amphibians. Common frog, toad and viviparous lizard have all been recorded on Surrey heaths, as have slow-worm and crested, smooth and palmate newts. Grass snakes thrive in the wetter areas. Britain's only poisonous snake, the adder, is relatively common, and is one of the few vertebrates to adapt to such open conditions. Two reptiles very much dependant on heathland, are the sand lizard and smooth snake.

Sand lizards are now found in a number of scattered locations in Surrey and Sussex, to some of which they have been reintroduced. They require old heather, which has begun to degenerate, from where they may obtain sufficient insect food, and bare, undisturbed areas of sand, in which to lay their eggs. Clearly, the maintenance of such habitat, free from fires, is essential to their survival in Surrey.

Smooth snakes are even more local, with the main concentration occurring around the Devil's Jumps at Hindhead. Without careful management, they may disappear.

Despite their barren and somewhat bleak appearance, the Surrey heaths are home to many insects, among the better known of which are several moths.

One of the commonest is the emperor, an attractive insect with large circular markings on the wings, looking like eyes. Although it has a variety of foodplants, heather is among its favourites. It is a fast flier, appearing in April and May. The eggs are laid neatly on the stems of heather and hatch into bright green caterpillars, covered in black bristles.

A species extending its range in Britain is the pine hawkmoth. A large grey moth with darker markings, its caterpillars feed on pine needles in late summer. A few are seen most years in Surrey, clearly in areas where pine is invading the heath.

The Archer's dart is a moth of some importance on the Surrey heaths. Away from Surrey, it is confined mainly to coastlands, except for a colony in Breckland. Its colour and markings are variable and several varieties have been named. The caterpillars feed in bedstraws and grasses, whilst the moth is on the wing in July and August.

Caterpillars of the silvery arches moth feed on docks, plantains and dandelion in the autumn. After hibernation, they seem to switch foodplants to the young growth of birches. It has a scattered distribution in Britain, the south-west Surrey heaths being one of its main areas.

A light greyish coloured moth, the miller, is on the wing in May and June. Its caterpillars, found from June to September, feed on birch and alder. As such, it is more frequently found on heaths than in woods, although it is not common anywhere.

Purple moor grass provides the foodplant for the marbled white spot, whereas a range of grasses and sedges are used by the silver hook. This latter species is widespread in Britain, but prefers bogs and fens. In Surrey, it has been recorded in a number of localities, including Thursley and Wisley.

The larger heathland bogs are home to a mysterious moth, called the marsh oblique-barred. Recorded in several places across the country, two were trapped at West bog, Thursley in July 1984. Nothing is known about the early stages of this insect, so its foodplant remains uncertain.

Far more common are the fox moth and four-dotted footman. Fox moth caterpillars appear in large numbers in some years, the creatures eagerly feeding on heather. They are covered in thick tawny hairs, which can irritate the skin. The caterpillars of four-dotted footman are hairy black. Although they will feed on heather in captivity, in the wild their food is algae growing on heather. Algae is also the foodplant of another heathland moth, the scarce footman.

The argent and sable moth is somewhat variable in numbers in Surrey, whilst the grey scalloped bar is rather rare. A few are seen at Thursley each year, although its main area of population is the New Forest. Rare but occurring regularly, is the autumn rustic, whose caterpillars feed on heathers, willows and grasses.

One of Britain's rarest moths, the shoulder-striped clover, is found on a number of heaths in Surrey, namely Chobham, Pirbright, Horsley and Thursley. Its foodplants are cross-leaved heath, sand spurrey and the seedheads of bog asphodel. A daytime flier, it is most regularly seen over south-facing slopes near the Thursley bog, and is under serious threat from heath fires.

A low, brisk-flying moth, rather dingy in appearance, is the waved black. Although now widespread throughout Britain, especially on Surrey heaths, this species was once known only from the City of London. This seems even more strange as its caterpillar feeds on various bracket fungi which grow on birch and pine.

The list of moths found on Surrey heaths is enormous, running to several hundred species. These are among the more interesting. The following occur in Surrey, and are restricted to heathland by their choice of heathers as foodplants; true lover's knot, heath rustic, beautiful yellow underwing, ling pug, narrow-winged pug, horse chestnut and annulet.

Among the butterflies, between thirty and forty species may be seen on Surrey heaths, out of the total British complement of seventy. Many of these are equally at home in other habitats, such as woodland and grassland, but the heaths do support specialist species too.

The grayling, a cryptically marked brown butterfly, can be regularly seen on the wing during July and August. It is particularly fond of sunning itself on bare ground. Various grasses are used as foodplants by the caterpillars, especially the hair grasses and couches.

Much more restricted to heathland, and very much part of the Surrey scene, is the silver-studded blue. Variable in colour and markings, the caterpillars of this small butterfly feed on broom, bird's-foot trefoil, ling, bilberry and the flowers of gorse.

The underside of the wing is the most colourful part of the green hairstreak butterfly. This is bright green in colour, whilst the upperside is dull brown. Once again, its foodplants include gorse, broom and ling.

Apart from these few species, all others can be found elsewhere, although many grassland ones, like the small, large, Essex and dingy skippers are frequently encountered.

Perhaps most outstanding among the invertebrates on many heaths are the dragonflies and damselflies. A high proportion of British species are found on Surrey heaths, particulary where the ground is dotted with small bog pools. Although their larvae are aquatic, this group are included here, as the adults are frequently seen flying over the heathland. Of particular importance for dragonflies is the Thursley National Nature Reserve, believed to be among the best European sites for this group.

Various common species may be seen on the heaths, including the brown hawker, emperor dragonfly and the banded demoiselle. The emperor is our largest hawker dragonfly and the one least likely to be seen away from water. The banded demoiselle is a truly spectacular insect, its wings bearing a bright blue metallic band.

Cross-leaved heath

The highlight among Surrey dragonflies is the white-faced darter. For scarce species within Britain, Thursley is the only British locality south of Cheshire where it is found. With a wingspan of two inches, and body black and red in colour, this restless species is the emblem of the Surrey Wildlife Trust. Although never flying far, it is difficult to approach. It settles on heather around the sphagnum pools in which it breeds, and can soar high into the sky if exceptionally disturbed.

Less rare, yet mainly restricted to Surrey and a few other parts of the south-east, is the brilliant emerald. Often found some distance from water, and with a wingspan of over three inches, this insect may be seen between June and August.

Even larger is the golden-ringed dragonfly, with a wingspan of four inches. It flies low over land and water between May and September, often along predictable routes. Heather is frequently used for perching when at rest.

Grasshoppers and crickets are more often heard than seen. For this reason they are not easily overlooked. Preferring open areas with relatively low vegetation, heathland provides ideal conditions.

Some species found are common, such as the common green grasshopper and common field grasshopper. Others are more restricted, particularly the large marsh grasshopper, found only on peat bogs. Recorded attempts have been made to introduce this species to some areas, although it has probably become established anyway. Relatively common in localities like Thursley is the bog bush-cricket.

Assassin bugs are a large family of insects, mainly confined to the tropics. As their name suggests, they are predatory insects feeding on other species. Of the six species found in Britain, the heath assassin bug, a brownish-black creature, is common and widespread on the Surrey heaths.

A plant bug, *Odontoscelis dorsalis*, occurs on heaths, especially in west Surrey, due to the presence of its foodplant, common storksbill. Elsewhere, it is a coastal insect. It is light brown in colour, with spiny legs and a hairy appearance.

Another bug, *Globiceps woodruffii*, found at Thursley, has been recorded at few other sites in Britain. Thursley provided the first record of the species, so it is from here that its description originates.

The green tiger beetle, around 13mm long, is one of the best known insects of our heathlands. Bright green, it has a pale spot on each wingcase. It hunts on the ground, but quickly takes to the air if disturbed. Its larger relative, the wood tiger beetle, is also a Surrey heathland species, despite its name. Darker in colour, it is rather rare.

The Apion genus of beetles has 84 representatives in Britain, several of which are feeders on leguminous plants like gorse. Several are therefore found on Surrey heaths, including *Apion ulicis* and *Apion miniatum*. These species belong to the group of true weevils, or snout beetles. The head has a long forward-facing section, to the end of which are attached the two antennae.

Among the rove beetles, a group which is largely predatory, *Staphylinus caesareus* is a rare species found on the Surrey heaths. Between 18mm and 25mm in length, it is a striking insect with black body, red wing cases and patches of golden hair on the abdomen.

Paederus beetles are conspicuous due to their bright colouration. Four species occur in Britain, of which at least one, *Paederus littoralis*, is found on local heaths. They run about in the summer with their abdomen erect, usually on sandy ground near water, on sunny days.

Heathers are host to a small beetle, *Lochmaea suturalis*, found in some locations. Many other species of beetle are known from our heathlands, but generally through their association with trees like birch and pine. A few are dung beetles, so are not restricted to this habitat.

Bees and wasps are abundant on heathland, largely due to the ease with which they can dig nests in the sandy soil. A species confined to sandy heathlands and coastal dunes, is the large orange and black *Ammophila sabulosa*. Wasps of this type have characteristic abdomens which are very narrow in front, and end in a club shape. The female insect makes a vertical or sloping shaft in the ground which ends in a bulbous chamber. She does not live in the burrow whilst it is under construction, and takes extreme care in choosing the site. After flying over the burrow to orientate herself, she flies off to find a single caterpillar as prey. This is put into the burrow, after stinging it, to make it immobile. Several stings are often necessary, and some caterpillars even need a vigorous bite in the neck. After laying an egg on the caterpillar, sand grains or stones are used to close off the burrow. This action ensures that the wasp grub has live food readily available when it hatches from the egg.

Of the hunting wasps, many types frequent heathland. *Astata boops* preys on crickets and grasshoppers, whilst *Ammophila pubescens* attacks larvae of butterflies and moths. Weevils are the target of *Cerceris arenaria*, and flies fall prey to *Crossocerus quadrimaculatus*. These are just some of the examples of wasps which use paralysis to keep prey alive and fresh, for their young.

Some bees are parasitic on others, especially *Nomada rufipes*, a common species. *Nomada baccata*, a parasite of *Andrena argentata*, a solitary ground- nesting bee, is rather rare. These parasitic species, more like small wasps in appearance, lay their eggs in cells made by the solitary bees. When their larvae hatch, they consume the food intended for the rightful occupants.

A wide variety of spiders are found on Surrey heaths. Several of these prefer the habitat, rarely being seen elsewhere. In the wetter places, *Clubiona phragmitis* may be found. Whilst generally living in low vegetation, such as ling, the female constructs an egg sac retreat in higher vegetation, like the flowerheads of reeds.

More common and much smaller (around 4mm) is the related *Clubiona trivialis*. A yellow to reddish brown species, it prefers exposed situations on heather and gorse, where it may be seen throughout the year.

54

Agroeca proxima is widely distributed on dry parts of the heaths, often bordering woods. Also preferring dry conditions is the 3mm long *Scotina gracilipes*, found on, or below heather.

Common among mosses and grasses, especially in damp places, is *Zora spinimana*, a light brown spider with two black stripes along its body.

Both sexes of *Xysticus sabulosus* are adult in autumn, where they may be found among heather. Uncommon in Britain, this is an attractive spider, basically black, but with many white markings. Also found in similar habitats is *Oxyptila atomaria, Evarcha fulcata* and *Evarcha arcuata*. Whilst *E. falcata* is common, *E. arcuata* is limited in distribution but often common on Surrey heaths. Another relatively rare species is *Aelurillus v-insignitus*.

Pardosa nigriceps is a common dark brown spider, found both on grass and heather at ground level, and in bushes. The Pardosa genus is largely found running on the ground, where it may also be seen bathing in the sun.

Similar to Pardosa is the local *Xerolycosa nemoralis*, which is found on the chalk hills as well as heathland. Seen in summer, it is basically black, with a pink line along its centre.

A rare species found at Thursley among moss is *Euryopis flavomaculata*. It does not make a web, but is a hunter of ants and other small arthropods. *Tetragnatha extensa* does build a web, but with few radii. An elongated spider, it is able to stretch itself along the stem of a plant, usually in damp places.

Keeping close to the ground among heathers, *Araneus quadratus* spins a web up to 40cm in diameter. Found in late summer and autumn, this common species is a colourful chestnut and white. Equally colourful is the yellow, brown and black *Mangora acalypha*, abundant on Surrey heaths.

Uloborus walckenaerius is one of only two species of spider in Europe which lack poison glands. To avoid their prey making an escape, they wrap it securely in silk after capture, spending up to half an hour doing so. Thickly covered in white hairs, this species is restricted to a few heathlands only.

Particularly found on the flowers of cross-leaved heath is *Thomisus onustus*. The females are variable and changeable in colour, helping them blend with the flowers on which they wait. Pink, yellow and white are possible, as are any combinations of these colours. It is restricted to heathlands in the south of England.

Of the closely related harvestmen, *Phalangium opilio* is the most likely to be found. It is common, and has legs up to 54mm long.

It is only possible to hint at the variety of insects and spiders living on Surrey heaths. Some heathlands have become nature reserves, whilst many are still under the control of the Army. Although the latter undoubtedly cause disturbance to some wildlife, much continues to thrive alongside the military exercises.

If the delicate web of life unique to heathlands is to survive, action needs to be taken to halt destruction of this fragile habitat. It may seem that most of west Surrey is still heathland, but much has been lost. In 1804 there were 55,400 hectares of heath in the county. By 1983 this had fallen to 5,901 hectares – a decline of 89%. Once Surrey had more heathland than any other county but, with a sharper decline than anywhere else in Britain, we now have less than one-third of that found in neighbouring Hampshire.

ABOVE: Bracken on heathland. LEFT: Dogwood – an invasive shrub of chalk grassland and RIGHT: Raft spider. (RS)

Scrublands

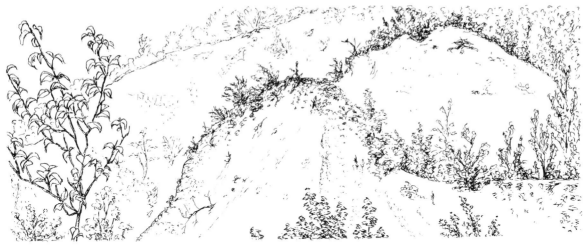

Scrub is a transitional habitat, occupying a stage in the natural succession from open habitats, such as grassland and heathland, to woodland. It is formed from a variety of small trees and shrubs, which may be of a range of different sizes, from a few inches to many feet in height.

Whilst grazing animals occupy grasslands or heaths, scrub is given little chance to develop. Constant nibbling by animals like sheep, cattle and horses is effective in controlling scrub invasion. If these animals are removed, rabbits are able to continue effective grazing if present in large enough numbers. This can be seen at Weeting Heath nature reserve in Norfolk, where the short turf of the heath is maintained solely by rabbit grazing.

In Surrey, rabbits were effective in preventing scrub development on the Downs for some time after most other grazing had ceased. The introduction of myxamatosis however, virtually wiped out the rabbit population in the 1950s.

A reasonably rapid growth of scrub followed the cessation of grazing. By the time the Conservation Corps (now Conservation Volunteers) was formed in 1959, the scene was set for what has now become a regular task – scrub bashing.

Clearing of scrub is necessary to preserve grassland and heathland habitats which are rare and support interesting plant and animal communities. Scrub also supports an interesting community, of which birds are the most obvious constituent.

Originally, many people felt that all scrub should be cleared. However, the practicality of doing so makes this an unlikely event and the intrinsic interest of the scrubland habitat, an undesirable one. The transitional nature of the habitat nevertheless warrants active management.

The first task of the Conservation Corps took place on Box Hill, a site important for its chalk grassland. It is logical, therefore, to aim to maintain grassland in areas such as this, where it is of high value. The initial cutting was followed by subsidiary cutting to deal with regrowth, which occurs in much the same way as in coppicing.

Continuation of regular cutting, whilst possible, is not a good use of volunteer effort. This is much better employed in tackling new areas. A recent innovation has been to graze areas with animals (largely sheep) during the winter. A parallel increase in rabbit grazing prevents major regrowth, so allowing volunteers to work elsewhere. On other sites where grazing is difficult, experiments into the selective use of herbicides have been made.

Grazing of heathland presents more problems due to the open nature of the ground. Here, both birch and pine scrub are a problem, requiring vast amounts of effort to clear. Birch, of course, regrows unless the stumps are treated, but pine does not. Seeding is intense though, so the main methods of control are to cut the larger trees and pull up the smaller ones.

Ideally, to preserve the wide variety of wildlife in Surrey, some mosaic of scrub and other habitats is desirable. As scrub grows taller much of its usefulness for nesting sites is lost. Different birds live at different heights and require varying amounts of cover, so the greater range of ages and species present, the better.

A rolling system of management, as seen on Bookham Common, is desirable. ·Here may be found three main habitat types – woodland, scrub and grassland. The scrub is clearly moving out from the woodland to colonise the grassland. As it develops, the scrub is turning to woodland, as well as seeding into more grassland areas. Management aims to cut out the areas of tall scrub, allowing them to regenerate as smaller scrub. The small growth is then cleared from the grassland to the benefit of that habitat. In this way, a wide range of ages is maintained and no overall loss of any of the habitats occurs.

In other areas, a different approach has been tried. At Park Downs near Banstead, scrub was cleared on a mosaic basis. Patches of scrub were cleared each year, between which areas were left. The result is rather like a chess board. An important factor in this type of management is that the corners of each area always adjoin, or are close to, those of similar habitat. This allows scrub creatures to move easily from one patch to another; similarly with grassland species.

Sharp edges to scrub can be detrimental to wildlife. Many species depend on naturally occurring lower bushes. Normally, where natural regeneration occurs, small bushes will tend to be on the edge, as these are younger plants seeded out from the adjoining shrubs. When clearing scrub, the edge effect can be lessened by pollarding, rather than removing, those bushes nearest the edge.

Scrub on the chalk downs is often dominated by hawthorn, although dogwood may be commoner in some places. Wild privet is also common in Surrey, with buckthorn, guelder rose, spindle and wayfaring tree being important components. These areas are also colonised by small trees, including birch, ash, whitebeam and beech. In some places yew is also common, its dense canopy shading out all plants beneath. Around rabbit warrens, elder may be locally abundant, whilst wild clematis scrambles over everything.

Scrub birds come in a wide range of shapes, sizes and habits. In Surrey, pheasants are often found in scrub, being most easily detected by the loud calls of the males. Some areas of land were planted up with snowberry in the past to provide cover for these birds, where they were reared for shooting. This tenacious alien plant has now escaped from these pheasant copses to form areas of scrub itself. However, it does seem to suit pheasants, although they are now found almost everywhere in the county.

Where some wet ground exists near more mature scrub, another gamebird, the woodcock, may be found. Although generally thought of as a woodland bird, woodcock can often be disturbed among the taller birch scrub on sites such as Headley Heath. They also like young plantations, which, in their early stages, are more or less like scrub.

Turtle doves, common summer visitors to Surrey, are perhaps our most attractive doves. Apart form their beautiful markings, they also have the most soothing call of any. They will live in a range of habitats, but mostly in the more rural parts of the county, away from suburbia. Often they nest in thorn bushes on the downs and commons, in places like Bookham and Banstead, but also in heathland scrub, as at Frensham.

Nightjars may be found in light scrub and young plantations. Like all ground-nesting birds, they are liable to considerable disturbance from loose dogs.

This century has seen a phenomenal increase in the number of magpies in Surrey. Part of this may be due to the reduction in gamekeeping in the county, but much can be put down to their relatively new-found scavenging methods of feeding. They are now tremendously common everywhere, posing a serious threat to other birds, whose nests they may raid for eggs. Their own nests are long, dome-shaped affairs, entered through a hole. They are often conspicuous in early spring in the tops of the taller scrub.

Although never so rare as the magpie, a reduction in persecution has also led to a considerable increase in the number of jays. These have now invaded all the scrubby areas of the county, so long as there are a few taller trees in which they can perch. Like the magpie, the jay is also a great predator of other bird's nests, particularly those of the blackbird and song thrush.

Rather like the magpie, the long-tailed tit builds a dome-shaped nest. Theirs is far smaller and more delicate, the outside often decorated with spiders' webs and lichens. Inside, thousands of feathers provide comfort. These beautiful pink, white and black birds prefer rural habitats and are great lovers of scrub. They are common throughout the county, although subject to fluctuations in numbers bought about by severe weather. In winter, they may often be found in parties, either with other long-tailed tits, or other species of tits, searching the scrub for insects.

Wrens will live anywhere there is adequate low cover, but may be common in scrub, particularly if it is young and dense. They are secretive birds, not often seen, but frequently heard. Despite being so small, they have one of the loudest voices of any scrubland bird.

Stonechats are more typically found among the gorse on heathlands, but also make use of some scrub and young plantations where these are near to heaths. The increased tendency to move into these areas may be due to losses of their preferred habitat.

A rather fussy bird when it comes to selecting areas of scrub for nesting, is the nightingale. From studies at Vann Lake reserve (where it has now disappeared) it seems to prefer scrub which is around the two metre level. It requires cover to be fairly dense and will sing even when well concealed from view. Because of these preferences it is able to benefit from both management and lack of it. If rotational scrub cutting is practised, then it may remain in the area as there is likely to be scrub of the correct height somewhere. If no clearance is done, then it may simply move from area to area depending on the height of the invading bushes. Whatever the case, there is a strong tendency for nightingale numbers to fluctuate at any one site.

Although publicity emphasises the song of the nightingale, that of the robin is probably just as melodious even though it may be given in rather short, loud bursts. Very common, robins are strictly territorial, probably actively defending an area of about an acre. Usually they will sing from the topmost branches of trees growing higher than the surrounding scrub, where their red breasts can be displayed to potential territorial invaders, to the best effect.

Song is certainly the best way of locating grasshopper warblers. These secretive birds make a reeling call which can be heard up to a kilometre away if the level of background noise is low. They prefer dense, tangled vegetation, with the occasional higher bush from which to sing. Generally they prefer scrub around three years old, so will move around an area if rotational scrub management is practised.

A loud songster, typical of Surrey scrub, is the blackcap. These birds will live in dense thorn scrub, or the equally impenetrable scrub of sallow. The species is named after the black cap of the male. The female has an orange-brown cap.

Garden warblers are even more frequently found in scrub than blackcaps. Both species may nest in close proximity to each other. They generally arrive later in the spring, but are common summer visitors to the county. Favoured localities include Bookham Common and Walton Heath.

Lesser whitethroat are also common during the summer, nesting in scrub on both downland and commons. Generally secretive, they prefer the taller scrub of the county. Living in any scrub is a close relative, the whitethroat. At the end of the 1960s, this species suffered a dramatic decline due to problems of crossing the drought-stricken Sahel region of west Africa, on its annual migrations.

Another two warblers, almost identical in appearance except for the colour of their legs, are the willow warbler and chiffchaff. Willow warblers have a descending trill song which is distinctive. It is a commonly heard sound of scrub, where this bird will occupy relatively early pioneer growth. Chiffchaffs utter a repetitive two-note call, sometimes for considerable lengths of time without a break. They also make good use of scrub, generally nesting in dense bushes only a metre or so from the ground. Areas which also have a few tall trees are favoured, as these are used as songposts.

Another species quick to invade new scrub growth is the dunnock. Common everywhere in Surrey, it is again most easily located by its song, this time somewhat reedy. Less commonly found in these habitats are greenfinches and goldfinches.

Areas of scrub, particularly dense ones, also provide shelter for a number of other creatures. especially rabbits, foxes and badgers. In an area like Brockham Limeworks, the homes of all three species may be found. To avoid disturbance, it is important to know the locations of such species before any scrub clearance takes place.

Some important plants may also be found in scrub areas. Where invasion is relatively recent, species like cowslip and hairy violet may survive on the Downs, or ling on the heaths. Plants such as the white helleborine may also grow, sometimes in profusion, whilst fly orchids also seem to like a little scrub.

Despite its intrinsic interest, there is still too much scrub in Surrey. It is a habitat which is unlikely to become as endangered as chalk grassland or heathland, so needs to be controlled. However, with sensitive management, control can lead to a greater variety of both wildlife and landscape.

Brockham Lime Works. (KB)

ABOVE: Scrub invasion at Brockham Lime Works. (KB) BELOW: Birch
scrub invading heathland surrounded by Scots pine. (KB)

ABOVE: Heathland with some scrub invasion. (KB) BELOW: Scrub
engulfing the hillside at Frensham Common. (KB)

Still Waters

Ponds and lakes are a beautiful, productive and vital part of the Surrey countryside. Unfortunately, many are no longer in the condition where they can support life.

Before Man came along, many ponds and lakes would have come and gone naturally. In some parts of the country large lakes developed as a result of geological conditions. In Surrey, many stretches of water probably developed where streams and rivers were accidentally dammed by fallen trees or the activities of creatures like beavers. Other areas would have been permanently waterlogged due to geology, topography and other local features, some the result of springs.

There is a natural tendency for ponds to silt up, with the invasion of plants. The remains of dead aquatic plants and leaves of overhanging trees slowly build up a base of organic matter, which leads to the depth of water decreasing. This allows other plants like reeds to move further into the pond. These help in the drying out process and are followed by small shrubs, then trees. Eventually, the pond may become a woodland.

When the impact of Man was tiny, such losses would not have mattered a great deal. Another pond was probably being created elsewhere. However, once Man began to develop the land and intensify agriculture, he found ways of draining the land.

At one time ponds became of great importance to the farmer. A pond in the field provided conditions suitable for stock to drink, whilst at the roadside it allowed carts to be washed and travelling animals to be watered. Not only were ponds deliberately created for these purposes, but their constant use kept down encroaching vegetation, so they did not dry out.

In some areas, ponds would hold water without much effort because they were either on the clay, the water table was high enough, or they were fed by springs. Others needed to be lined, normally using puddled clay.

These days, more animals are kept indoors and those outside often have piped water. Consequently, farm ponds have fallen into disuse. Often they have been fenced out of fields and left to grow over. Even worse, they may have been used as rubbish dumps. Some areas have kept them. Although not necessarily used for their original purposes, many are well maintained. South of Capel are a series of farms on which many ponds have survived, giving some indication of the frequency with which they must once have occurred.

Man did not only create ponds in connection with agriculture. Some were developed in order to provide the power to operate medieval iron industry hammers; some by the abbeys to raise fish for food; others may once have been peat diggings; many were ornamental. Whatever their origins, they all provided a home for at least some wildlife.

Whilst recent years might have seen the infilling of many unwanted ponds, Surrey has benefitted (in some ways) from Man's need for drinking water, sand and gravel. Many reservoirs have been built around London this century, whilst old mineral workings have often developed into lakes by simply being left to fill with water. The latter usually develop a more natural appearance as the shallower parts become colonised by plants, and willows move in around the edge. However, although rather stark and open in appearance, reservoirs have proved their value as havens, particularly for wintering birds.

For some species, the size of the pond can be an important factor determining its use. Whilst mallard are often found on the smallest village pond, for instance, great crested grebes need larger expanses of water, big enough to support the birds and their family, and deep enough to dive in.

Some ponds have been affected by pollution. This can take many forms. Oil accidentally or deliberately discharged into a stream will accumulate on the surface of a pond, whilst agricultural chemicals can find their way into water if used in large quantities. Clearly, any pollution has seriously adverse effects on the wildlife of the pond.

Despite their attractive appearance, tree-lined ponds are not always good habitats. A few trees around the edge is fine, but too many will considerably increase leaf fall into the water. If the south bank is shaded, light will not reach the water, preventing aquatic plants photosynthesising. Without plants no animals can live in a pond, as there is no food and little oxygen. Even the carnivores need herbivores on which to feed somewhere down the food chain.

When the Surrey Wildlife Trust took over Nower Wood in 1971, all the ponds were heavily shaded in this way. One of their early tasks was to open up the south banks. Over a few years, the ponds changed from being dark and lifeless into ones filled with plants, insects and fish.

The Nower Wood ponds are an example of those dug for ornamental purposes. Nower Wood was once a wild garden attached to Headley Court. The ponds, which were surrounded by plants like rhododendron, not only looked attractive, but supplied water to the gardens and stables through an elaborate plumbing system. Although this has long ceased to function, four of the five ponds remain intact, the fifth having developed into a marsh.

Few birds use the ponds at Nower Wood, perhaps because the trees make if difficult to fly in and out. However, mallard are usually present, as are moorhens. A particular feature of these ponds and many others in Surrey, is the mandarin duck. Originally from China, mandarin escaped from wildfowl collections, setting up home in the south of England. Gradually they have spread from their original area of escape along the river systems. They may now turn up on almost any pond in Surrey. They especially favour wooded areas, as they nest in holes in trees. Now rare in its native country, the Surrey mandarins form a significant part of the species' world population.

Mandarin were first seen flying in the wild in 1929. Shortly after, some pinioned birds were introduced to a small pond in Cobham. These are thought to form the basis for the large breeding flock on Virginia Water and the surrounding Windsor Great Park. In some winters, flocks of more than one hundred are seen there.

At Godstone, two other Surrey Wildlife Trust reserves present two different types of freshwater habitat. Bay Pond is a large lake, held back by an artificial dam built around 1611. Godstone Reservoirs, on the other hand, are areas of water occupying worked-out sand pits.

Bay Pond is relatively shallow, although of sufficient depth to allow great crested grebe to dive. It is fed by a stream which brings in large quantities of silt. By 1985, the levels of silt had built up to considerable depths, necessitating a major dredging operation. To reduce the need for future dredging, a large hole, known as a silt trap, has been dug on the inflow to the lake. During the winter, when the stream is in full flood, the waters first pass through a large bed of reedmace before reaching the lake. This is expected to filter out any chemicals that may otherwise pollute the water.

Although reedmace may help to filter water before it reaches the pond, it does cause considerable problems in management. If left, the beds become extensive, rapidly taking over new areas. Control involves wading waist-high in the water and pulling up the plants. However, birds such as the moorhen, Canada goose, mute swan and reed warbler use these beds for nesting, so some areas must be maintained.

The amount of decaying matter produced by plants like reedmace and common reed can be enormous. Consequently, many species of wildlife act as cleaners in this zone. Many are invisible to the naked eye, but some, like the water louse, *Asellus aquaticus,* may reach 25mm in length. Looking rather like an aquatic woodlouse, these crustaceans are particularly common in weedy ponds. They scavenge on all kinds of decaying organic matter and also eat algae. In winter, they are usually found in pairs, although a closely related species, *Asellus meridianus,* is not. When in pairs, the male carries the female beneath him, although for what reason is uncertain.

Flatworms may also be found on the bottom in this zone. Whilst identification of species is not easy, these fascinating creatures play a useful role in consuming dead animals. They can scent food from some distance and feed by sucking up body fluids through a long feeding tube. They are the simplest animals to have a central nervous system.

The fringe zone may also support other plants like marsh marigold and yellow iris. Together with the reeds these may provide suitable sites on which emerging insects can dry their wings.

Once they emerge, the life span of an adult caddis fly is very short. After almost a year under water, the flying insect, somewhat mothlike in appearance, flies over the water from which it came. They eat little or nothing at this stage, mate, then die. During the larval stage, they remain concealed within protective cases which they make from sticks, leaves, sand grains and other objects. They move around the bottom of the pond thus concealed, retreating fully inside if danger threatens. They feed almost exclusively on plants. Some species of caddis fly can produce scents, which are believed to be of value in mating.

Around the edges of many ponds, toad or frog spawn may be found. Each year, when they awake from hibernation, these amphibians make their way to the ponds in which they were born. Quite how or why this is done is not known, but it may continue for many years. Often, this leads to some ponds developing a reputation for 'being good for frogs or toads'. They seem to find their way even if the pond has dried up. Neither are they deterred by obstacles like roads. During these annual movements, at such road crossings, many meet their death. In some places, volunteers with buckets go out on appropriate evenings to help them across the road, whilst a few ponds, like that at Shalford, are now graced by special road signs on their approaches.

The males usually arrive at the pond first. They are easily detected by their loud, croaking calls. Often, in the clamour to mate, a toad or frog will grab the first thing it finds, be it stick, another male, or a female. If another male is accidentally held it makes a release call, on which the would-be suitor realises his mistake and lets go. Once a female is found, the male climbs on her back, holding her tightly until she has spawned. He fertilizes the eggs externally, before the familiar jelly absorbs water and swells around them. Whilst frog spawn is produced in a large, free floating mass of between 2,000 and 4,000 eggs, toad spawn is deposited in long strings, entwined around submerged plants.

Also fairly common in Surrey ponds are newts. They do not attract a mate by calling, but practice an underwater courtship. When the male smooth newt, for example, finds a female, he first touches her along the side with his nose. After a chase, he moves in front of her to display his crest and wiggle his body about. Fertilization of the eggs takes place internally. The male deposits a sperm packet into the pond which is collected by the female in her cloaca. The other two species, the palmate and great crested newts, fertilize the eggs whilst pressing their cloacal openings together.

Great crested newts are the least common of the three species, but are widespread across Surrey. They are much larger than the other two species – about 15cm long. Their skin is covered with small holes through which they secrete a substance distasteful to other creatures, as a means of protection. A pond in Epsom has now been designated a Site of Special Scientific Interest as it supports one of the largest populations of great crested newts in southern England.

In the open water may be found floating plants like the yellow and white water lilies. The yellow species is the commonest in Surrey, although the white is the most frequently planted. Water lilies present their large, showy flowers above the surface, whilst broad, waxy leaves are able to shed water, thus remaining buoyant. Beneath the water, the leaves are more lettuce-like in appearance. The stems end in strong roots, anchoring the plant to the pond bottom. Water lilies can reproduce rapidly, choking lakes with their growth. In some areas, such as Vann Lake near Ockley, a number have to be pulled up at regular intervals.

Far smaller, but commonly floating on the surface of ponds, are the tiny duckweeds. Measuring only a couple of millimetres across, this plant can quickly colonise the entire surface, turning it a bright green. They often appear on ponds even after they have been newly dug. They are possibly carried there on the legs of birds, or on the bodies of amphibians and mammals. Common duckweed is the most frequent species, even turning up in puddles and water tanks. Duckweeds can survive in filthy water, even if heavily polluted with farmyard manure, suggesting a preference for a high organic content. The tiny leaves (more correctly called thalli) produce small 'roots' reaching down a short way into the water. In spring and summer they reproduce by budding from small slits in their sides. Duckweed is capable of flowering, but rarely does so in Britain.

Looking rather like a mossy duckweed is the far rarer water fern. Waterfowl are thought to be responsible for spreading this plant from garden ponds where it was originally planted. An American alien, water fern sometimes rapidly increases after colonising a pond, only to vanish again a few years later. This is probably because, being a subtropical plant, it is unable to tolerate severe winters. Over the years it has turned up in a number of sites in Surrey.

Pondweeds of the Potamogeton group are now far less frequent than past records suggest. The commonest species is the broad-leaved pondweed, which needs basic or neutral waters. At Young Pond in Nower Wood, this species reappeared after the pond was opened up and acidity levels reduced.

Far commoner in the west of the county is bog pondweed. This species lives in bog pools and ponds where the water is acidic. Like other pondweeds and floating plants, the leaves serve as platforms for many aquatic creatures.

A particularly interesting group of water plants are the bladderworts. These plants, which reproduce both vegetatively and by fruits, float totally submerged beneath the surface. They are most common in ponds deficient in minerals, such as those found at Thursley.

Their branches support numerous small bladders which have neat circular openings at one end, with small bristles surrounding a trapdoor. Small creatures are attracted to the plants by mucilage glands near the entrance to the bladder. When they touch the sensitive hairs around the trapdoor it opens inwards. The sudden inrush of water draws the creature with it. The door closes, the animals eventually die and are absorbed. This way the plant makes up for nutrient deficiencies in the water. Both the lesser and greater bladderworts are rare in Surrey, but the former has been known at Thursley since at least 1850. The greater bladderwort has been recorded from a pond in Epsom.

Surrey ponds support probably one of the most endangered plants in Europe. The starfruit, once known from more than fifty localities in Britain, is now confined to one pond in the Leatherhead area. Even there it has not been seen for several years.

A member of the water plantain family, it flowers from June to September. It grows on the muddy edges of gravelly ponds where the water level falls in early summer. Some people say it grows best on ground regularly trampled by geese! Although always erratic in appearance, it has vanished from a number of former haunts in Surrey. Unless it reappears in this one last pond, its only hope of survival in Britain may lie with artificial propagation.

A plant rare in Surrey, but found in a couple of the more acidic ponds, is pillwort. Rather grass-like in appearance, this mat-forming fern lives in the shallower muddy waters at the edge of ponds. At the sites where it is present, it may become abundant during dry years when the water level falls.

Carnivores of the pond include water boatmen, great diving beetle and water scorpion. The commonest water boatman is *Notonecta glauca,* which is widely distributed. They will often be seen resting upside-down at the surface. They also swim upside-down, using their long rear legs like a pair of oars. They are boat-like in shape and are made buoyant by a bubble of air held against the front of the body by four rows of hairs. Water boatmen will attack a variety of creatures, even fish larger than themselves.

Alder (RST)

The largest and best known beetle of the pond is the great diving beetle. Olive brown in colour and 35mm in length, the adult insect has a yellow margin around the wing cases and thorax. During mating, the male uses several suction pads on his feet to cling to the body of the female. They are able to swim together for hours at a time. Like water boatmen, they are excellent swimmers and ferocious carnivores. On summer evenings they may indulge in nocturnal flights, sometimes mistaking wet greenhouse roofs or wet roads for a stretch of water.

Water scorpions, which look rather like dead leaves, lie on the bottom of the pond, near the bank. If handled, they feign death. Water scorpions lay their eggs in the spring, just below the surface, amid masses of plant material. Each egg is supplied with a number of thread-like tubes which allow it to obtain oxygen.

Perhaps the most commonly encountered pond insect is the pond skater. Around 15mm in length, there are ten species in Britain. Their lightweight bodies and long legs enable them to run across the surface on the surface tension. They are scavenging carnivores, largely living off the dead and dying insects which fall on the water.

Of the fish, probably the best known of all is the three-spined stickleback. Common everywhere, these lively little fish grow to about 5cm. Early each spring, the male, which develops a red throat, red belly and blue eyes, starts to defend a territory. A nest is then built, using algae and weed, cemented together by a sticky solution, originating from the kidneys. The male defends his territory against other males, eventually attracting a female by a zig-zag courtship dance. After the eggs have been laid and fertilized, he defends them until they hatch, fanning them frequently. He continues to look after the young when they are born, gathering them up in his mouth if they venture too far during their early days.

Another common fish of Surrey ponds and lakes is the handsome perch. The dorsal fin, which helps fishes maintain balance, is spiny and reddish coloured in this species. Perch are found in a variety of sizes up to five pounds in weight. Generally, they are far smaller. The smallest specimens feed on water fleas, which live among water weed in shallow water. Larger ones eat insect larvae whilst the largest consume small fish.

Stew ponds were very much designed with fish in mind. As we know, religion forbade the consumption of meat on Friday, but fish were acceptable. The abbeys therefore set about making sites where they could rear fish. Two ponds constructed on Epsom Common were the property of Chertsey Abbey. The smaller pond survived and is still used for fishing today, largely by small boys. The other, however, was drained earlier this century.

In 1976, volunteers of the Surrey Wildlife Trust, Surrey Bird Club and Epsom Common Association tackled one of their biggest projects to date. The original Great Pond had been five hectares, but only 2½ could be restored – a gas main had been laid across the centre in the intervening years. Only weeks after the flooding, amphibious bistort had colonised the pond. Moorhen, mallard and little grebe also moved in.

Other stew ponds in Surrey include Frensham Great and Little Ponds. Much larger in extent, they were owned by the Bishop of Winchester. The Great Pond is much disturbed in summer by thousands of visitors. Whilst many also find the Little Pond, its more isolated location has allowed it to preserve its bankside vegetation well, providing nesting sites for birds like reed and sedge warbler. Because of its draining during hostilities and subsequent loss of reed growth, reed warblers declined at Frensham Great Pond after the Second World War.

A rather rare plant in the county in general, sweet flag is particularly common at Frensham Great Pond. A native of south and east Asia, it was first recorded in the area at Headley in Hampshire in 1666. From Tudor times it was in demand for medicines. It is said to have uses for treating flatulence, dyspepsia, anorexia and gall bladder disorders. It now grows on many ornamental ponds, plus the whole length of both the Wey and Arun and Basingstoke canals. It rarely flowers in this country and has never been known to fruit.

Mayfly larvae are abundant at Frensham Great Pond. There are several species of mayfly, adapted to living in different types of water. In ponds, some cling to vegetation beneath the surface while larvae, whilst others occupy the silted bottoms. The larvae (or nymphs) are active mainly at night and feed largely on vegetable matter. Most complete their metamorphosis in one year, some having at least two generations. Their brief aerial life usually makes itself known on evenings in later May or early June, when they appear over waters in vast swarms. They are easily recognised as they hold their wings erect when at rest. Also they are equipped with three (sometimes two) slender tail filaments.

Among the plants of Frensham Little Pond is the water mint, a common species of most waters throughout the county. Other mints occur in many places in Surrey, partly as the result of introductions in garden rubbish. Since the 1930s, however, the number of accidental introductions seems to have reduced considerably, in line with an increase in those appearing on rubbish tips. This is probably due to more organised waste disposal.

Over the last hundred years, northern Surrey has acquired a series of reservoirs to supply London with water. An earlier reservoir, built south of the Downs to supply water to the Wey and Arun canal near Cranleigh, is Vachery Lake. Once an important lake, it is in private hands, so difficult to observe.

Today's reservoirs fall into three groups. These are the Barn Elms reservoir at Hammersmith; a group near Staines; and another group close to Walton-on-Thames. Permits are issued to birdwatchers by the Thames Water Authority, enabling them to take advantage of these excellent birdwatching sites. No permit is needed to birdwatch at Staines Reservoir, which is crossed by a public causeway.

The Lambeth and Chelsea reservoirs (all part of the Walton group) have vertical sides, making them difficult for some birds to use. Some, such as Barn Elms, whilst being largely vertical, incorporate a shelf at water level, which is a great advantage. Among those built with sloping sides is the Queen Elizabeth II reservoir at Walton, covering 130 hectares and reaching a depth of 20 metres. It was completed in 1962.

Queen Elizabeth II provides an interesting example of how bird life can change along with habitat. When construction began, several diggings were started. These were puddled with clay before the Second World War stopped work. At this stage, two gravel pits were also in use, providing a range of varied wetland habitats covering 31 hectares. The surrounding area was farmed.

Construction did not recommence until the end of the 1950s. In the intervening period the area had become well known for its breeding reed bunting, yellow wagtail, redshank, snipe, little grebe and lapwing. Migrants were common on passage and smew regular in winter. When pumping was started to allow construction to continue, the shallower waters attracted little ringed plover. The developing bank provided shelter for roosting gulls as work proceeded.

By the time the reservoir opened, the equipment to pump water from the river was not ready, necessitating the transfer of water from neighbouring reservoirs, established since the early twentieth century. This led to a direct transfer of some of the life of the other reservoirs, including fish. Mallard, teal and great crested grebe soon took advantage of the new water. Later shoveler, tufted duck and pochard discovered the Queen Elizabeth II reservoir. Being the deepest of the Walton group, it is also the last to freeze over in winter.

Gravel pits are largely concentrated in north-west Surrey, particularly around the Staines, Thorpe and Chertsey area. Some of these provide temporary habitats only, as they are filled in shortly after use. Many others have been left in a flooded state, providing homes to a range of duck, grebe, moorhen and coots. As the vegetation develops around the edge, more reed-nesting species may be seen.

Some gravel pits have been developed for recreational use in recent years. Those at Send have been landscaped for sailing, but still remain attractive to birds. Near Chertsey, a group have been incorporated into Thorpe Park, a major theme park. This may have reduced the number of birds present in summer, but large numbers of tufted duck and coot still frequent the pits in winter.

At one time, Vann Lake near Ockley, a Surrey Wildlife Trust reserve, was an excellent site for waterfowl. Only as recently as the early 1970s mallard, tufted duck, coot, moorhen, mandarin and Canada goose were numerous. Today, this spectacular lake, built to power a linen mill which was never built, sits devoid of birds, in a steep, wooded valley. Almost certainly, this is due to a heavy presence of mink. Related to the otter, these 50cm long carnivores are a uniform, deep-brown in colour. They were first introduced into Britain as fur farm animals, which soon began to escape. They are now firmly established throughout Surrey, including both Vann Lake and Bay Pond reserves.

Mink are insatiable predators, often attacking water birds. It is said they frequently kill far more than they can eat, eliminating whole populations of birds and small mammals. Their normal food includes frogs, fish and water voles. Trapping has proved ineffective, so it seems likely many waters will continue to be out of bounds to birds for the foreseeable future. Although nocturnal in their native countries, naturalised mink are often bold in Surrey, coming close to people. However, there appears to be no truth in the rumour that they have attacked humans.

All of the birds once regular at Vann Lake are still quite common in the rest of the county. Mallard are undoubtedly the most widespread, breeding on almost any lake or pond, even in the centre of towns. In urban areas, where they are generally fed by the public, they remain tame. The situation in the countryside is different. Mallards on quiet woodland ponds can be difficult to approach, flying at the least disturbance.

Tufted duck have undergone a large expansion in recent decades. Once confined to large bodies of water, they now frequently occupy smaller ponds, even in towns. The black and white drake is most attractive, but even the females sport the brilliant yellow eye.

Gravel pits have played an important part in the expansion of this species. They will not colonise the pits until they have developed a reasonably rank surrounding herbage, in which they nest. Their food is mostly animal, especially the introduced zebra mussel, which is spread throughout the country.

Breeding of tufted duck in Surrey had not been proved until this century. In the 1920s, regular wintering occurred in east Surrey. Reservoir construction encouraged more to winter until, by the 1950s, it was one of the commonest wintering species. Breeding is now recorded on at least twenty waters annually and undoubtedly occurs on many more. In winter, most waters usually show an increase, the largest concentrations usually on Barn Elms Reservoir and at Thorpe Park.

Pochard, another diving duck, only occasionally breeds in the county. However, it is frequently encountered in winter, particularly on the reservoirs and gravel pits. When breeding does occur, it is usually on sites such as the Pen Ponds, in Richmond Park. They seem to prefer shallower water than tufted duck and are primarily vegetarian.

Coots require larger areas of water than the related moorhens, so are more restricted in their distribution. They are, however, common in the county, moving into many town lakes and ponds this century. The nests are often on the water, anchored in the local vegetation. Nesting practice can be clearly seen at haunts like Dorking Mill Pond.

In winter large rafts of coot gather on gravel pits and reservoirs, sometimes several hundred together. A largely vegetarian species, coot are bottom feeders. During their dives, they harvest plant material, which is consumed on the surface. They may also be observed grazing grassland.

Unlike many other waterbirds, numbers of moorhen have remained largely stable this century. They breed on a range of waters including large lakes, small ponds, gravel pits and watercress beds. Moorhen nests are relatively easy to find, so are subject to heavy predation. This necessitates a long breeding season, often from March to August, during which several repeat clutches are laid. In winter, small concentrations of up to 50 birds may be seen at localities such as Pen Ponds.

Among other waterbirds are teal, small duck which nest in thick cover. They are only occasionally recorded nesting in Surrey, but may form sizeable concentrations in winter. These are generally at sites like Island Barn Reservoir, but smaller flocks may be spotted at places like Ash Vale gravel pits.

Gadwall are similarly scarce in the breeding season and barely more frequent in the winter. Most birds turn up around the Barn Elms reservoir, although odd individuals have been recorded at places like Holmethorpe sandpits, Redhill and Pen Ponds.

Wigeon winter on the reservoirs, as do a few shoveler, scaup and goldeneye. Birds like red-throated diver also turn up from time to time, although indication as to when or where cannot be given with certainty.

Great crested grebes have benefitted greatly from changes in Surrey this century. The creation of gravel pits has provided them with many more areas of open water large enough to breed on, allowing the population to grow dramatically. However, some of its original sites, such as Gatton Park Lake at Redhill, are still among the most important localities in the county.

Gatton Park also provides a home to a flock of Canada geese. These birds were first introduced to Britain over 200 years ago. The first recorded wild breeding in Surrey was at Godstone in 1905. By 1930 they had established themselves at Gatton, where a large flock still exists today. Now, Canada geese breed on a number of waters in the county.

Away from these and outside the breeding season, flocks may turn up almost anywhere. They regularly move around the county and sometimes commute into sites on a regular basis.

On waters where both species are present, mute swans are dominant over Canada geese, frequently threatening them with wings arched over their back. At Bay Pond, Godstone for instance, mute swans and Canada geese usually nest at opposite ends of the pond. Unfortunately, swans have declined in number in recent years through lead poisoning from discarded fishing weights. However, it is to be hoped that the banning of these weights will allow a recovery.

Herons, being large birds, may be thought immune from the effects of severe winters. Yet, when ponds freeze over, they have no way of reaching food, so can easily starve. Throughout the year, herons may be seen in ones and twos across the county, whilst groups may turn up in autumn and winter on the larger lakes. Individual birds sometimes venture some way from main water bodies.

Herons are communal nesters, generally building in trees, but are surprisingly difficult to spot. Numbers have declined at a number of locations over the past thirty years, the largest colony now being at Fort Belvedere, Virginia Water. This colony is of ancient origin.

Secretive birds of Surrey ponds and lakes include the water rail and kingfisher. The water rail has been recorded in some localities in most months, but is largely a rarely seen winter visitor.

Kingfishers are more frequently seen, both on still and moving water. Like herons, they are badly affected by severe weather. They are limited in the number of breeding sites by the requirement to have banks into which they can burrow. At Vann Lake an artificial bank was built by Conservation Volunteers, whilst elsewhere natural sites are often found. Outside the breeding season they may be seen darting across a number of ponds. I have even seen one at Dorking Mill Pond, just behind the High Street.

During this century there has been a tremendous increase in the number of wintering gulls in Surrey. This has been especially noticeable since the 1920s, when these birds started to turn up away from their previous haunts on the Thames. Largely this expansion has been due to their adaptation to sites created by Man. Rubbish dumps, sewage farms and even playing fields provide ample supplies of food, whilst the reservoirs provide night-time shelter.

The most noticeable species in terms of numbers has been the black headed gull. It now seems odd to think that it was only in 1912 that the sighting of twelve black headed gulls at Frensham Great Pond was exceptional. Flocks roosting on the reservoirs can now run into hundreds of thousands, these birds commuting in and out every evening and morning. During the day they move far out to feed, across the county, well beyond the Mole and Wey gaps, which are used as flight paths. Although a few birds are present throughout the year, ringing recoveries have shown that many of our wintering black headed gulls come from the Low Countries and West Germany. The similar Mediterranean gull also turns up from time to time in black headed flocks. One was seen for several winters in succession at Epsom Common.

Lesser black backed gulls are larger than black heads. They generally occur in smaller numbers although roosting flocks can reach more than 1,000 in strength. As well as those which winter in the county, many more pass through on autumn migration, stopping off on large playing fields, race-courses and so on. Similar numbers of greater black backed, herring and common gulls winter in Surrey. A seabird which has not taken advantage of inland wintering sites in the same way is the kittiwake, of which only a handful are seen each year.

For an inland county, a surprising number of waders also turn up in winter, or on passage. A few find their way to the more rural lakes such as Vann Lake, but the majority go to the reservoirs, gravel pits or sewage works. Over recent years, at least one half of Staines Reservoir has been fully or partly drained, providing exposed mud attractive to this group. Whilst larger water bodies like reservoirs and gravel pits are likely to remain, many of the smaller ponds will, or already have, dried up.

At Forest Green, a plaque indicates that this pond won an award during the Save the Village Pond campaign. In Newdigate in 1984, the village and the Surrey Wildlife Trust got together to clean out an old pond near the church. Apart from his work at Epsom Great Pond, perhaps the most important campaign to save ponds in Surrey has been undertaken by Bob Forster in the Tadworth area. The number of ponds restored under his guidance shows just how many more remain derelict, if only we look hard enough. The greatest contribution anyone can make to save the many species of wildlife which depend on still waters, is to go out and restore their nearest pond.

Forest Green Pond – Save the Village Pond winner. (KB)

ABOVE: Roadside cart pond, Newdigate. (KB) BELOW LEFT: Bogbean
and RIGHT: Bog asphodel. (JEGM)

73

ABOVE: A farm pond in Shackleford. (KB) BELOW: Village pond,
Cranleigh. (KB)

ABOVE: Town pond, Dorking. (KB) BELOW: Vann Lake reserve. An
artificial pond made by damming a stream. (KB)

75

ABOVE: Sunset over Papercourt Gravel Pits. (KB) BELOW: Recently disused brick clay pit, now flooded.

Deep alder carr, Moor Park, Farnham. (KB)

ABOVE: Boardwalk providing access to Moor Park. (KB) BELOW: Thursley Common Bog – outstanding Surrey wetland site and the only nesting site for the curlew. (KB)

78

ABOVE: Female mallard and family. LEFT: Drake mallard. RIGHT: Yellow iris.

ABOVE: The river Wey wends its path through Thundry Meadows reserve. (KB) BELOW: Tranquil scene on the Basingstoke Canal at Frimley Green. (KB)

Rivers and Streams

Most of Surrey lies within the catchment of the River Thames, which passes through the northern part of the county. Into this flow both the River Mole and River Wey. In addition, the River Tillingbourne, which rises in the Leith Hill area, is a tributary of the Wey, joining it near Shalford. Small areas in the south of Surrey drain into the River Arun. North River, which passes through Vann Lake reserve, becomes the Arun further downstream. In addition, a section of south-east Surrey comes within the catchment of the Medway, *via* the River Eden. Whilst most references are to rivers, much similarly applies to streams.

Among the best studied of these rivers is the Mole, partly as a consequence of its geological and geomorphological features, partly because it is convenient for London schools and colleges. Rising near Rusper in West Sussex, it flows through St Leonard's Forest, then roughly north-westwards, to join the Thames at Molesey. The 487 square kilometre catchment area includes a selection of geological strata, including Weald Clay, London Clay, Bagshot Beds, Chalk and Greensand. For most of its route the river is rural. It does, however, flow through the Gatwick Airport complex and through the Leatherhead and Molesey conurbations.

The development of Gatwick Airport and the adjacent Crawley New Town have had a marked effect on flooding from the Mole after heavy rain. Before development of this area, water would have been gradually absorbed through the ground, finding its way into the river over a long period. Following the covering of much of this upstream area with concrete, run-off is much faster, causing rapid changes in flow after heavy rain. This can give rise to widespread flooding along some stretches of the river. Those waters which inundated Molesey during the 1968 floods were increased in their impact by development of the floodplain around that town, bringing dwellings within a short distance of the riverside.

Much information about the Mole has been collected by the Nature Conservancy Council, when the river was chosen as one of those in the south-east worthy of study. Much of the data produced was gathered from field observations of the whole river, but the records of fish, which include a fair number of species, came from anglers.

Whilst all fish occur naturally, fishing clubs have stocked some stretches too. Perhaps the most widespread species is perch, which only seems to be absent from the upper stretches of the river. Reports of bleak, a brilliant silver coloured fish, come mainly from the middle stretches to the north of Cobham, where some water has been channelled off to fill Painshill Park lake.

Bream occurs along most of the river. It is ideally suited to the Mole, preferring slow-moving waters, where it can feed on weed and small invertebrates. There is much splashing during spawning, which takes place in marginal weedbeds, during May and June. A much smaller related species, silver bream, is found in the Leigh area.

Carp is also found throughout most of the Mole. It feeds largely on plant material, but also takes small invertebrates living on the river bottom. It belongs to a group of highly successful fish which are able to tolerate quite stagnant waters.

Chub feed on insects near the surface, sometimes in small shoals. Large chub are more territorial and will eat other small fish. The much smaller dace feeds on a mixture of plant and animal matter, keeping near the surface. It spawns in gravelly sections of rivers, so is at home in the Mole, where, despite the sometimes murky, muddy looking water, the bottom is often gravelly.

Roach are common in the river, feeding omnivorously near weedbeds. They spawn from April to June, each female laying up to 10,000 eggs. These stick to plants and hatch in a few days. The similar looking rudd feeds throughout the water, from riverbed to water surface. Tench live at the bottom of the river, overwintering in the mud. Between May and July they breed, each female being capable of laying up to 900,000 small, green eggs.

Pike, predatory fish with strong teeth and jaws, have been reported from several stretches of the river. They generally lurk unseen amongst vegetation. Their prey, depending on the size of the fish, can include frogs, water voles, ducklings or other fish such as the miller's thumb.

Although these fish records all relate to the River Mole, much the same can be expected of the River Wey. This water originates as two streams, one flowing mainly from the chalk near Alton in Hampshire over Upper Greensand and Gault Clay to Tilford, the other from the Lower Greensand at Hindhead to join it at Tilford. Beyond this point, it continues on the Lower Greensand for a while, until it cuts through the chalk near Guildford. The rest of the journey is over Bagshot Beds and London Clay to the Thames at Weybridge. Between Godalming and Weybridge the river was made navigable by the construction of the Wey Navigation canal in the 17th and 18th centuries. This in part uses the canalised river, but elsewhere employs a parallel artificial channel.

A fish not mentioned, but found in limited numbers in both the Mole and Wey, is the brown trout. This prized species is also to be found in the Tillingbourne. In some places the rainbow trout, a North American species, may be caught. Both species have had their numbers maintained by stocking.

Aquatic plants in the River Mole are rather poorly represented. The upper stretches display an almost complete absence of them. North of Gatwick, plants like branched bur-reed, reedmace, common water plantain and common water pepper become more frequent. These then occur intermittently as far as Brockham. In places, yellow water lily also grows. Around the Box Hill stretch, plants such as arrowhead can be found. Beyond Box Hill, aquatic plants again become rare although some reed canary grass and branched bur-reed grow in places.

Between Stoke D'Abernon and Cobham, much change has taken place. Whereas the river once flowed through water meadows, part of it has been canalised to accommodate the M25. Around Cobham, a few emergent plants again appear including spiked water milfoil. Relatively little in the way of aquatic plants are found beyond Cobham.

The bankside vegetation of the Mole is also rather uninteresting. Mostly it comprises a range of nettles, brambles, thistles and grasses. In places the banks are grazed to the waterside, otherwise the most typical species are purple loosestrife, tansy, hemlock, great willowherb and Indian balsam.

The southern branch of the Wey passes through an area of generally poor, sandy soil. However, the aquatic vegetation is good and varied throughout this stretch. Water starworts and spearworts are frequent, as are broad-leaved pondweed, common duckweed and Canadian pondweed. Along the banks may be found various willowherbs, purple loosestrife, tansy, hemp agrimony, marsh woundwort, forget-me-nots, watercresses, common comfrey, branched bur-reed, hemlock and skullcap.

Commoner on the Wey than the Mole, is orange balsam. A native of North America, it was first noticed here in 1822, on the River Tillingbourne at Albury. Later it was recorded from the Wey at Guildford. Since then it has reached the Thames and moved upstream along the Wey and Tillingbourne, this being possible by its seed propelling mechanism.

Another alien plant is the monkey flower, naturalised from gardens. Although found on both the Wey and Tilingbourne, it does not appear to spread. It is still found largely in the areas where it was present in 1931. It has showy, red-spotted, yellow flowers. The seeds, which develop in a small capsule, number about 150. They are dispersed by water, or on the feet and feathers of birds.

The land alongside the northern branch is largely used for agriculture. Little plant life has developed in the upper reaches of this stretch of river, which is shallow and narrow. Watercress, procumbent marshwort, celery leaved buttercup and blue water speedwell are the most frequent species. The last of these is rather rare in Surrey. Beyond Farnham, other plants appear, such as branched bur-reed and various waterweeds.

Wild angelica

The banks along this part of the Wey resemble those of the Mole, with a preponderance of nettles, thistles and grasses. A few typical bankside plants do, however, grow in places, including nodding bur-marigold. Woodland reaches the banks along other stretches, one of the most significant being at Moor Park, where a deep alder carr has formed.

After the two branches combine, there is little of special note to Godalming. The most interesting and comprehensive vegetation is found alongside the Thundry Meadows reserve. Elsewhere, even the aquatic vegetation is minimal.

Between Godalming and Guildford, the most southerly stretches of the Wey Navigation are encountered. Where the canal occupies a new cut, the river itself is left as a quiet backwater, often with a good vegetation. There is still little in the way of aquatic plants, but meadows alongside the river support plants like marsh marigold, various rushes and sedges.

Arrowhead, which first appears below Broadford, is the dominant aquatic here. Arrowhead produces different leaves at different times of year. The early leaves are submerged. These are followed by floating ones which are in turn followed by emergent leaves and flowers.

Unlike the River Mole, which is shallow and only used for a little canoeing, the River Wey between Godalming and Guildford is extensively used for boating and angling. In addition, it passes through the heart of Guildford, where much casual recreation takes place. This has a detrimental effect on the wildlife of the river, causing pollution and worn banks.

Beyond Guildford, the stretch of river to the Thames was the first to be canalised (in 1653). Often the river and canal are in different channels, sometimes up to half a mile apart. In many places the canal has the richest vegetation, except in towns. Some of the best vegetation on the whole Wey can be found here.

A Nature Conservancy Council survey in 1976 took samples at five localities along the River Mole, to determine the invertebrates present. The commonest creature encountered was the freshwater shrimp.

Despite their name, they are not true shrimps. They are, however, common and usually found under stones or on the surface of mud at the river bottom. Lightish brown in colour and about an inch long, they usually swim in pairs, the male carrying the female beneath him. They are mostly scavengers, feeding on decaying matter. Sometimes, they have been seen to eat another small creature, or even each other.

The female has a brood patch beneath the thorax, in which the eggs are carried. Once the young hatch, they may be carried around for a while too.

Next commonest were mayfly nymphs, closely followed by the wandering snail in the upper reaches. This snail is confined to soft waters, whereas *Bithynia tentaculata*, found on stones, weed and bogs, prefers hard water. Ram's horn snails also turn up in Surrey rivers. Oddly for snails, their blood contains haemoglobin, which makes it red.

Other molluscs regularly found are pea-shell cockles. There are several species, all of which are favourite food of fish and waterfowl, which consume them, shells and all. Less than 7mm long, the different species are hard to tell apart.

Freshwater oligochaete worms are common in Surrey. They often burrow into the bottoms of muddy rivers. This, together with the fact that they are almost colourless, can make them somewhat difficult to see. They feed on decaying vegetable matter, passing vast quantities of such matter through their bodies to obtain what they require, rather like earthworms.

Water mites are present in most stretches of river in Surrey. Rather like small spiders in appearance, they are only tiny, varying between 2 and 8mm. They are active creatures, swimming rapidly or climbing about among water plants. They feed on a variety of animal food including water fleas, midge larvae, worms and even other mites. Unlike spiders, which hatch into miniatures of the adults, young mites have only three pairs of legs. Some 200 species of mite are found in British water. Those most likely to be found in slow-moving rivers like the Mole and Wey, belong to the *Limnesia* group.

Of the dragonflies and damselflies, the most frequently seen along Surrey rivers are the large red damselfly and common blue damselfly. The small red damselfly may also be seen. All three species are on the wing from May to August. The banded demoiselle is also frequently seen. An attractive species, it has bright blue bands on its wings. I have found it to be particularly common on the well-vegetated stretches of the River Wey, south of Guildford.

Many of the creatures which live in rivers and streams have to find ways of not getting swept away by the current. Even where the current seems slow to us, this can be a problem if you are only a few millimetres long. However, the flow-rate reduces significantly as one moves from surface to bed of river. Many species, which live on the surface of stones and other objects on the river bed, are able to do so as the flow over these objects is minimal or non-existent. Because this quiet zone is only about one millimetre thick, these animals tend to have flattened bodies, like the leeches. The creatures have suckers at either end of their body, to hold them in place.

Other organisms employ suckers too. Among these are the blackflies. This group of insects can be a problem abroad, and even in Surrey there are species which bite a variety of birds and mammals, including humans. The adults lay their eggs in jelly-like masses on the edge of streams and rivers, using stones and plants as a base. When the larvae hatch they crawl into the water and attach themselves to a surface, normally in the fastest-flowing section. The larvae, which can occur in great numbers, sieve food particles from the water until full grown. Then, they spin a brown cocoon, still attached to the substrate. The pupa absorbs an excess of oxygen from the water, enabling the adult to be carried to the surface on hatching, in a bubble of air. It takes to the air immediately on reaching the surface.

An interesting feature of the River Mole at Leatherhead are the number of islands. Although not of any particular botanical interest, they do provide undisturbed sites for nesting birds, as they are inaccessible from the bank. Generally they are wooded, with much red campion and cow parsley. Whilst many of the birds making use of them are typical species of the town – blackbird, for example – this stretch does provide the chance to see all three species of wagtail, plus mallard, moorhen, little grebe, heron and kingfisher.

The River Mole supports many pairs of mallard, moorhen and mandarin. In addition, herons are regularly seen, although never breeding. Little grebe are also common, the wooded, secluded nature of some sections being particularly to their liking.

Although shy, kingfishers are relatively common along the River Mole. Again, the seclusion of many stretches must be greatly to their liking, although the steep, easily excavated banks are also important factors limiting their breeding sites.

The bird fauna is similar along the River Wey, both rivers also supporting some mute swans, tufted duck, Canada geese and water rail.

Along Surrey rivers the water vole may often be encountered. Burrowing into soft, muddy banks, this mammal is often to be seen 'plopping' into the water. They excavate extensive tunnels in which their families are raised. Food is mainly the roots and shoots of riverside grasses, which are also used to line the chamber in which the naked, blind and helpless young are raised. Their holes can often be located if a careful search is made.

Mink have already been covered in the previous chapter, although they are also widely distributed along the Surrey river network. Although occasional reports of otters are heard, they are almost certainly extinct in the county, the sightings most likely being of mink.

One of the major achievements of recent times has been the cleaning of the Thames, returning it to the quality it possessed several hundred years ago.

Above Teddington, the river has been clean enough to support most species of fish for all of this century, due to the work of the Thames Conservancy, formed in the mid-19th century. The tidal section has been restored more recently, completion only coming in the 1970s. Since then, salmon have begun to reappear after an absence of some 150 years.

A fish which needs both salt and fresh water, salmon swim away from the headwaters of the rivers where they are born, during their second year. After growing for a further year or two they leave our seas to cross the Atlantic. On their return, they swim back to the spawning ground from which they were hatched.

Until the start of the 19th century, these migrations were a regular feature of Thames life. Londoners even complained of having to eat too much salmon. They vanished in the Victorian era with the invention of water closets. The water-borne sewage was piped, untreated, into the nearest river, without a thought for pollution.

Salmon and most other fish disappeared from the Surrey stretches with this onslaught, which was only finally arrested after the Second World War. With its life-cycle broken, salmon had to be reintroduced to the headwaters of the Thames from 1978, when the water was clean enough. Since then, salmon have begun to return annually to the river, which is now one of the cleanest urban rivers in the world.

River life can be fascinating to study, particularly if note is taken of the adaptations each species makes to prevent it being washed out to sea. However, it survives on a knife edge, always under threat from accidental pollution. Oil or sewage may leak into the water, doing serious harm before it is identified. Alternatively, nitrates washed from farmland may cause rapid increases of some species which then swamp out others, or use up the total supply of oxygen.

River management can lead to the canalisation of rivers, in attempts to encourage water to move downstream and out to sea more rapidly. Apart from the visual impact, this type of management leaves little habitat for wildlife, as most trees and vegetation are removed. Clearance of some plant growth is, however, often necessary to keep channels open. Usually this can be done from one side of the river only, leaving vegetation on the opposite bank for the displaced animals.

With careful planning rivers can be used by all, whether for birdwatching, fishing, walking or boating. Even so, more research is clearly needed to monitor the effects of different activities on the river ecosystem and ensure the reconciliation of differing demands.

LEFT: River Tillingbourne, Abinger Hammer. RIGHT: A stream wends its way through damp birch woodland at Barfold Copse with abundant ferns. (KB)

ABOVE: The river Mole flows through open parkland near Betchworth,
(KB) LEFT: Small red damselfly, RIGHT: and blue pimpernel. (DAE)

ABOVE: Sheep grazing dip slopes of the North Downs. (KB) BELOW: Rough grazing near Dunsfold.

On the Farm

The Surrey countryside is so heavily wooded that it seems little of the county is farmed. Even so, some 40% is farmed or used for horticulture. Most of that land is not as intensively used as in some parts of Britain. Partly this is because many farms are run by business or professional people more for pleasure than profit. There are a few larger farms, usually under the control of managers. Another particular speciality of Surrey is the number of 'pick your own' farms, no doubt due to the large market from the county and London.

Despite this picture, recent decades have seen an enlargement in the size of fields, an increase in mechanisation and fertilisation and, in some cases, even aerial spraying. Rarely are fields of poppies still to be seen although, when fields are first ploughed after many years as pasture, they still appear in their thousands.

Beef and dairy cattle are a familiar sight in the county, especially the latter. Although there is a wide variety of soils, the large areas of clays to the north and south of the Downs are not really suitable for ploughing. Although some cereals may be planted on the greensand, its low fertility does not lend it to arable. In some areas, particularly around the Downs, fields may be larger than average, even big enough to enable several combine harvesters to work at once. The value of sheep has also increased more recently, although most of those that are to be seen graze on artificially fertilized areas.

The effect of fertilizer on grass can be clearly seen in winter. Looking towards the Downs, some places will support grass which is light brownish in colour, whereas large patches of bright green indicate the fertilized areas.

A few other crops may also be seen in the county. Unlike a few years ago, it is now no longer unusual to see patches of bright yellow dotting the Weald, as oil-seed rape bursts into flower. Neither is maize uncommon, being largely grown for silage. Other more unusual enterprises include dairy sheep and goat farming, or even deer farming.

Like other parts of the country, about half of Surrey's farmland is found on less than 10% of its farms. However, there is a proportionately higher number of small farms in the county. Also, the size of Surrey farms is about 60% of the national average.

All this may suggest that wildlife has a better chance of survival on a Surrey farm than one elsewhere. Whilst this is probably true, the amount of wildlife has been considerably reduced. Even relatively minor operations can have a marked effect, such as the replacement of old barns with modern ones. These old buildings often provided ideal places for birds like barn owls and swallows to nest. There are probably still plenty of buildings where swallows can gain access, but the larger spaces which are relatively undisturbed, required by barn owls, are certainly rare these days. One of the best areas for these beautiful birds is south of Capel, where a number of farms have preserved their old buildings. In one case, a pair regularly nests in a water tower. Recently, nest boxes have been made available to farmers who wish to encourage these useful birds onto their land.

Other problems faced by barn owls include poisoning by pesticides. Pesticides used to control small mammals can accumulate in these animal's bodies, but not necessarily in large enough quantities to kill them, before they are captured by owls. Owls, feeding almost exclusively on these mammals, can build up fatal levels of pesticides.

Another owl often found on Surrey farmland is the little owl. It seems to prefer areas of farmland adjacent to parks and woods, or along streams and rivers. A tiny owl, only 21 to 23cm in length, it is often to be seen in the daytime, when it perches prominently on fence posts or hedgerow trees. Despite their small size they are capable of taking prey up to the size of a half-grown rabbit, but more usually feed on smaller mammals and birds. Up to half their food consists of insects. Not native to Britain, little owls were first brought to this country from Rome. Those which formed the nucleus of the current Surrey population were probably released in Kent in the late 19th century.

Many other birds may be seen around the Surrey farmyard, including species like the house sparrow. They nest in a range of nooks and crannies, but always near to Man. In farmyards large colonies may build up in old buildings or haystacks where their large, untidy nests are characteristic. Able to adapt to food situations provided by Man, this bird can be a serious agricultural pest, especially in standing cereal crops before harvest. Flocks may also be seen in stubble after harvesting, or dust bathing in the farmyard.

Another pest on farms is the collared dove. Until the 1930s, these birds were restricted in Europe to Turkey, Albania, Bulgaria and Yugoslavia. Then began a spectacular population increase. By 1952 they had spread 1,600km across continental Europe. The first bird to arrive in Britain came in 1954. Clearly they found an ecological niche not occupied by any other species and quickly spread over most of the country. Collared doves are largely grain feeders, being especially attracted to farms, hen runs and pheasant rearing pens.

Even more of a pest, probably the worst bird pest species in the country, is the woodpigeon. Able to exploit green plant material as food, it was checked in numbers until the widespread planting of winter crops like turnips, kale, other brassicas and clover which are green throughout the winter. Together with ripening grain in July and August, farmland has become the main home of woodpigeons, which now use woodland mainly for roosting or nesting.

Another group of birds typical of agricultural land are the crows. Of these, the carrion crow is the most widespread, found throughout the county. It nests in a range of habitats, but always in single pairs. However, unlike a few years ago, when a single crow or pair could always be guaranteed to be carrions, and a flock in a field were jackdaws or rooks, we now see flocks of carrion crows as a matter of course in Surrey. This increase in numbers is largely due to a reduction in gamekeepering this century, the species previously being killed as it was considered a threat to birds' eggs.

Rooks have been persecuted by Man for centuries, usually without good cause. Although sometimes injurious to agriculture, this species is often of great benefit to farmers, as it includes large numbers of leatherjackets and other insect pests amongst its food. Even so, Surrey has certainly not been a good rook county, at least in this century, the species seeming to prefer places where the fields are larger, but still contain sizeable clumps of mature trees in which they live in noisy colonies. In recent decades the rook has certainly declined in Surrey, though not as the result of tree losses to Dutch Elm disease, as has been claimed elsewhere. Several rookeries have vanished, even though the healthy trees in which they were sited still remain.

Jackdaws also nest in colonies and are noisy too. Quite often the nests will be in holes in trees, but may also be found in a variety of other locations. They may sometimes be seen in fields with rooks, but often form large, single species flocks feeding on larvae of moths, spiders and other invertebrates.

Magpies, like carrion crows, thieve other birds' eggs as part of their food. Again they were controlled by gamekeepers until this century. In fact, it was quite recently when they began a major expansion, and are now to be seen in large numbers on Surrey farms. Their large, untidy nests may often be found in the hedgerows.

To many people, the hedgerow is an important part of the landscape. Much has been said about the losses of hedgerows with the introduction of larger farm machinery. Whilst the removal of any hedge will have a certain effect on the wildlife of the farm, some hedges are better than others.

It is the destruction of other habitats which has increased the value of hedgerows. In areas where there are plenty of woods and unimproved grassland, hedgerows would be less important. Most of the species they contain come from one or other of these habitats. As such habitats become rarer, hedges become more important.

Unlike the Midlands, where hedges were planted mostly at the instigation of a number of Enclosure Acts, dividing up large, open fields, those of Surrey are often woodland remnants left when the fields were cut from the original wood. Hedges formed in this way are often of considerable value for wildlife as they contain a number of the woodland species from the original wood.

For this reason, the system of dating hedges by counting the number of woody plant species in a 27 m section often does not work in Surrey. The method assumes that the hedge is initially planted as a one species hedge. New woody species, therefore, are assumed to invade every hundred years or so. A hedge with nine woody species would date to around the Norman conquest. Many hedges in Surrey contain this number of species, simply because the original woodland had several to start with.

Barn owls (RST)

Of course, some single species hedges have been planted, these usually being of less wildlife value. In addition to those hedges made from woodland remnants, the other old, species-rich hedges are usually those forming boundaries of ancient significance, particularly parishes.

Where hedges were planted, hawthorn was the species most often used. Two species exist within the county, the common hawthorn and the midland hawthorn. The former has deeply cut leaves and flowers with only one style. The leaves of the latter are indented less than halfway to the midrib and the flowers have two styles. Unfortunately, things are not that simple. The two species have widely hybridised, leading to a variety of different types.

Other frequent hedgerow shrubs are blackthorn, hazel, holly, field maple, ash and buckthorn. Of these, blackthorn is probably the most conspicuous early in the year, when it bursts into a mass of white flowers before the leaves make an appearance. Later in the year, the species is also well known for its dark blue fruits called sloes, used to flavour gin. Another early flowerer is hazel, the long yellow catkins of the male often being seen in January or February. Holly flowers later, between May and August, the flowers of the different sexes being on different plants. The greenish flowers of field maple also appear in May, as do ash and buckthorn.

Many spring flowers will be found in good hedges, although these are largely typical of woodland – primrose, lesser celandine and ground ivy, for instance. Lady's smock, more a plant of wet places, may be seen, especially if the hedge is bordered by a ditch. A member of the cabbage family, garlic mustard is a foodplant of the colourful orange tip butterfly, as is lady's smock.

A little later in the season, Surrey hedgerows become dominated by cow parsley. Less conspicuous, but present in large quantities is the cuckoo pint. As hawthorn bursts into flower, so do colourful plants like the red campion and the delicate, white-flowered, greater stitchwort.

By May, the hedgerows are much in demand for nesting sites of many small birds. Typical of these are seed eaters like the chaffinch, omnivores like the yellowhammer, insect eaters such as dunnocks and, where there are higher trees in which to nest, goldfinches. Other birds including blackbird and robin are common, as are wrens.

From a wildlife point of view, the more bushy and overgrown a hedge is, the better. However, overgrown hedges take up large areas on a farm and overshadow crops. Most often, Surrey hedges are mechanically cut, which often results in their bottoms becoming gappy. A laid hedge, unfortunately now rare in Surrey, is not only stockproof but good for wildlife. Often, where management has been lacking, only a few bushes remain to mark the line of the hedge.

Many of the plants which farmers call weeds can be better described using a term coined by the Butser Iron Age Farm in Hampshire – arable competitors. Like the crops with which they compete, they do not like much competition, so do best in cultivated soil, where they can grow quickly, flower and die, all in one year.

A typical plant of such conditions, frequently seen around the edges of fields where the crop is often less well established, is scarlet pimpernel. Much rarer is the blue pimpernel found in a scattering of localities on the chalk. In at least one place a hybrid between these species has been reported.

To most people poppies are typical of cornfields. These days this is less so, although they will often dominate some fields, where they have recently been ploughed for the first time. More often, they are to be seen in the disturbed soil alongside new roads. Still widely distributed across Surrey are both the common and long-headed poppies. These are distinguished largely by the shape of their seedheads. The rough poppy, only recorded in a handful of localities in Surrey, is again identified by its seedhead, which is covered in stiff bristles. Quite frequently the lilac-coloured opium poppy may be seen, especially where marginal land is ploughed for the first time. This happened particularly in the Headley and Fetcham areas in 1942. Another member of the poppy family, sometimes seen alongside hedges on agricultural land, is greater celandine.

Another yellow-flowered plant frequent on arable land in Surrey, is charlock. Although common on chalk and clay soils, it is less frequent, but still present, on sandy soils. Frequently found in the county are completely, or almost completely hairless plants – an unusual form.

Although never as common as in some other counties, the cornflower is now extremely rare. A plant with thin leaves, almost grasslike, and a bright blue, dandelion-like flower with a reddish centre, this plant is now only occasionally seen in arable fields, due to the efficiency of modern grain-cleaning methods. The plants were once known as hurtsickle, because their tough stems blunted reapers' sickles.

Corn marigold, a troublesome plant of arable land, has not been eliminated quite so effectively. Its seeds are able to remain viable for a number of years, permitting sudden explosions of the plant when conditions are right. It thrives on sandy soils, so is restricted to west Surrey and the greensand ridge.

Many other plants, particularly of the daisy family, are to be found around the edge of fields especially. One of these, pineappleweed, smells strongly of pineapples when crushed. The flowerheads comprise only the yellow tubular florets as found in the centre of daisies, so look rather like a daisy without any white 'petals'. Despite the smell, the plant is not edible.

A plant with medium-sized daisy-like flowers and reduced narrow leaves is scentless mayweed, again common in the county. Looking very much like it and locally abundant in Surrey, is stinking chamomile. It was said by one writer in the 19th century to be called poison magweed, probably because its acrid juice often badly inflamed the hands of harvesters. Corn chamomile, another of this group of similar-looking plants, is now quite rare in the county, particularly favouring chalk. Its most frequent location is between Headley and Ashtead.

A practice which has become increasingly controversial in recent years is stubble burning. Many people have devised guidelines on this, including the National Farmers Union. These advise the ploughing of strips around the edges of fields to act as firebreaks, thereby protecting hedges, and the importance of advising authorities of what is about to be done. Of course, none of these precautions is able to prevent the destruction of wildlife in the stubble, unable to get away. In particular, there are liable to be large numbers of invertebrates. The only way these losses could be prevented would be to find alternative uses for straw and stubble.

Many insects do, inevitably, cause farmers severe problems. Craneflies, common indoors on damp autumn evenings, start life as leatherjackets. These grey, cylindrical maggots, about 20mm long, live in the soil, causing considerable damage to plant roots. Many other insects, such as ladybirds, are beneficial, living off other species, often pests.

Fields where burning takes place may also be home to birds like partridges or even harvest mice. If the burn goes too deep, beneficial creatures such as worms may be destroyed, alongside harmful ones like slugs.

Other mammals may also be seen on Surrey farms, including those also found in woodlands. Therefore, roe deer may be seen along with hedgehogs, foxes and badgers. Molehills may frequently be seen in fields, often in large numbers, but their occupants are rarely encountered. Less welcome mammals include field mice, house mice and rats.

Wildlife on the farm has to be capable of surviving the constant upheaval caused by ploughing, sowing, pesticides, herbicides and burning. Some species are better at this than others but, if only these were to survive, our flora and fauna would be the poorer.

In recent years, some farmers have loaned their stock at certain times of year, to bodies like the National Trust, which then use them for selective grazing on the Downs.

The Surrey Wildlife Trust took the alternative approach a few years ago, when it purchased its Thundry meadows reserve, along with a herd of cattle to graze it. Looked after by a volunteer, the cattle are sold for beef as on a commercial farm, realising a small, but regular profit.

For wildlife on the farm, schemes like this are clearly beneficial. Another is the Farming and Wildlife Advisory Group. A few years ago, representatives of conservation and farming bodies in the county met and formed an advisory group. Since then, a full time advisor has been appointed.

Future events may also have a bearing on wildlife, including possible changes in the EEC Common Agricultural Policy. In the past, wildlife has often suffered at the hands of farmers. Often, this has been essential if the farmer is to make a living. Let us hope that in the future, ways will be found to enable farmers to make a reasonable living whilst protecting wildlife. Surrey has fared better than most counties, but there is still room for improvement.

ABOVE: The arrival of prairie farming, Dorking. (KB) LEFT: Orb web spider. (DAE) RIGHT: Roman snail. (DAE)

94

Living with Man

Throughout this book we have seen how Man has modified the Surrey countryside. In some cases the changes have been beneficial to wildlife, such as the effects produced by coppicing on woodland plants. In other situations, Man's activities have allowed a group of species to adapt to survive in an artificial environment, sometimes becoming pests. Obviously the biggest change Man has made is the building of structures to satisfy his needs. Those common in everyday life are houses, shops, factories, offices, roads, churches and less obvious artefacts include playing fields, cemeteries, mines and parks.

Today, buildings cover a considerable part of Surrey. Most of the former northern part of the county has been developed and incorporated into the London Boroughs. In some areas, the dense networks of terraced houses bordering treeless streets, leave little room for wildlife, although even there many plants will push their way through cracks in the pavement.

Further out, the suburbs of London developed in places like Ewell, Cheam and many others. Here, homes are mainly sited in large gardens and the streets are lined with trees. Similar areas exist around most Surrey towns, whilst in the countryside, the gardens are even larger.

Although the amount of management each individual garden receives varies, the complete network of gardens which winds its way through the suburbs makes up what is effectively a vast nature reserve. The gardens are all relatively undisturbed and border each other, providing areas of shrubs, trees, grassland and flowers suitable to a variety of species.

Many creatures live there, among the most obvious of which are birds. These include familiar species such as the house sparrow and blackbird. The male blackbird is one of the most attractive of garden birds, glossy black with an orange bill. The hen is brown with a brown bill. They feed on a variety of foods, including many different invertebrates and fruits. Often blackbirds are to be seen doing battle with an earthworm. The neat nest is usually built in a hedge, so this species is often predated by cats. They normally rear two or three broods in a season. Apart from cats, blackbirds are often under threat from cars, due to their habit of flying low across the road.

Another thrush found in Surrey gardens is the song thrush. Like the blackbird, it has a musical song, but is far less common and avoids heavily built-up areas. It has a special preference for snails, getting at the juicy contents by smashing the shells on the path or rockery. Mistle thrushes, which are larger normally only frequent larger gardens where they enjoy eating fruit put out on the ground.

More easily recognised is the robin. In Europe, this species, like the blackbird, is a shy woodland creature. Here it is often exceptionally tame, nesting in odd corners in the garden shed.

Much shyer is the dunnock which, whilst frequently visiting gardens, is less noticeable due to its drab colouration. It will often nest in garden hedges, such as privet, so common in Surrey. However, its habit of nesting low down does hamper its success rate. In winter, it will eat food put out for birds, although it prefers to feed at ground level, rather than from a bird table.

A range of different finches make use of Surrey gardens. The chaffinch is undoubtedly the commonest, nesting in larger gardens or in the suburbs where many gardens adjoin. If the garden contains thistles and other similar plants, goldfinches may visit for seeds in the autumn. Greenfinches, natives of the woodland edge, are most often seen in winter, feeding on nuts and other foods supplied by residents. A similar bird, but smaller and more streaked, is the siskin. Since the 1960s, this species has been an increasingly common one in Surrey gardens, particularly feeding on nuts contained in orange net bags. Most colourful of the finches is the cock bullfinch with bright red breast and cap. Whilst this species sometimes visits bird tables in winter, it will be better known for its preference for eating plant buds, sometimes causing damage to currant bushes in winter.

Another group of common garden birds are the tits. The more common are undoubtedly the blue and great tits, which also make use of nestboxes. However, the coal tit may also nest sometimes, preferring conifers – often, a single conifer will do. Some larger Surrey gardens also support a pair of long-tailed tits, whilst both marsh and willow tits will visit more wooded gardens in winter.

Pied wagtails often appear on lawns, running about, flicking their tails, whilst feeding on insects. They are also frequently seen on roads, where they pick insects off the surface. If the garden contains a pond, there is an even greater chance of seeing one, as they take advantage of the swarms of insects which the water attracts. Pied wagtails nest in holes, raising up to three broods between April and July.

Because of the wooded nature of many Surrey gardens, a whole range of woodland birds may be seen. These include occasional visits by all three species of woodpecker, or a glimpse of a treecreeper working the tree trunks. Nut hatches may also be seen on garden trees in the county, or even on bags of peanuts in winter.

A bird present around the house all year is the starling. Although more gregarious in winter, when many more birds arrive from overseas, numerous starling families nest in holes in both trees and buildings.

Of course, house martins also make use of buildings for nesting. Usually their nests, built of mud, are constructed under the eaves. Quite frequently house sparrows will evict house martins once they have finished building their nests, taking over for their own use.

Another bird using a similar type of nest is the swallow, although theirs are more frequently in old farm buildings. They do, however, hunt for insects over gardens and are often to be seen gathering together on telephone wires in the autumn, before departing for Africa.

More rarely, swifts nest under the eaves too, although they seem to prefer old buildings, where they nest in cracks. Never landing except to incubate their eggs, swifts collect together nesting materials on the wing, cementing them with saliva.

Many birds visit Britain in winter from more northern latitudes. These include a great number of waterbirds, but also two thrushes – the fieldfare and redwing. They will often be seen in Surrey gardens, especially if there are berry bearing shrubs, or fruit is provided for them to eat.

Putting food out for the birds usually, sooner or later, attracts a grey squirrel. Once they have discovered such a food source, they often become pests, quickly consuming everything provided. They have even been seen to take peanuts from hanging metal baskets, by eating the basket as well!

Much more popular among the mammals are hedgehogs, a frequent visitor to Surrey gardens. Despite their widespread presence (indicated by the number killed on the roads) hedgehogs are

ABOVE: Badger. CENTRE LEFT: Hedgehog and RIGHT: house sparrow.
BELOW LEFT: Tawny owl and RIGHT: wood mouse.

PLATE V

Surrey woodland butterflies: ABOVE LEFT: grizzled skipper; RIGHT: pearl-bordered fritillary. CENTRE LEFT: brown hairstreak; RIGHT: white admiral. BELOW LEFT: silver-washed fritillary; RIGHT: small pearl-bordered fritillary.

PLATE VI

not often seen unless bread and milk are supplied. Mainly insectivorous, they can be heard on summer evenings, grunting and rustling around the hedge bottoms.

Even less often seen is the mole, although its presence is usually given away by unwelcome molehills on the lawn. Only if the expanse of lawn is large are these animals likely to be present, when their tunnels provide an excellent aeration system for the ground.

Sometimes a wood mouse or yellow-necked field mouse will find its way indoors. If not, it is quite likely that one or both of these species will be present in the garden. House mice are much more closely linked with Man and can do tremendous damage. Especially, this is caused by their need to shred paper (and other materials) with which to build their nests.

Like house mice, the brown rat is an alien pest species. It followed Man to all parts of the world from Asia, arriving in Britain early in the 18th century. It is most common among rubbish and sewers, but may also include houses, where it can cause considerable damage.

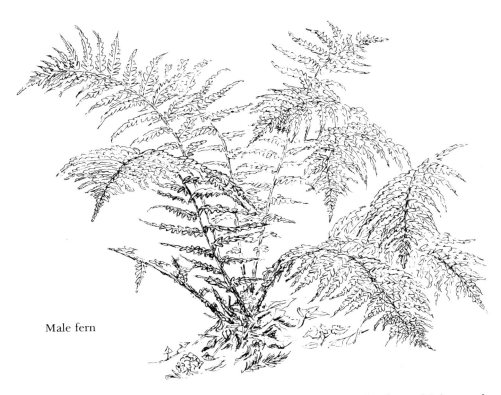

Male fern

Increasingly common among the range of garden mammals is the fox, which may be found throughout the county, living in close proximity to humans. Not only does it live in gardens, where it may breed under sheds and feed from dustbins, but it is also found along railway lines, on wasteground or even in derelict buildings.

Some larger gardens also support a badger sett. Preferring areas where there is little disturbance, badgers sometimes live quite close to towns, several setts even surviving within a few hundred yards of Croydon High Street. However, their survival has been threatened in 1986 by plans for new flats.

A particular feature of many Surrey gardens, especially in the west and centre of the county, is deer. Although rarely seen, roe deer make excursions into gardens at night, even quite close to town centres, usually to feed on rose bushes.

Bats are another group of little known mammals, despite several species living in houses, even modern ones. All bats are protected by law, although there is no need to evict them from lofts as they do no damage. Very little is known of the distribution of the various bats in the county, but a Surrey Bat Group was founded in 1985 to study these creatures and advise housekeepers who have bats in their houses.

Insects provide food for bats and, in their many different forms, are common in the garden, especially where insecticides are not extensively used. Among the best known are the butterflies. Many species will appear from the surrounding countryside if nectar-rich plants are grown. One of the best plants is buddleia, also known as the butterfly bush.

Early in the year, brimstones may often be seen after they emerge from hibernation in evergreen shrubs or ivy. Small tortoiseshell also hibernate, emerging early in the year. Usually they hibernate in dark places like the corner of sheds, but may sometimes attempt to do so indoors. In such situations this is often unsuccessful as they awake during the winter when the heating is turned on. Egg laying takes place in April and May on stinging nettles, a plant also used as food by peacock butterfly caterpillars.

Orange tip butterflies may also be seen occasionally in gardens. Their caterpillars feed on a range of plants that are members of the cabbage family, especially garlic mustard and lady's smock. Other butterflies which depend on this family are the large white and small white. Both go under the general term cabbage white and can be pests to gardeners. Sometimes an ichneumon fly called *Apanteles glomeratus* lays its eggs inside large white caterpillars. These hatch into grubs, up to 100 feeding inside the body of the caterpillar. As their survival depends on the ability to obtain fresh food, they do not attack the vital organs of the caterpillar until they are themselves mature.

Of the remaining butterflies likely to visit Surrey gardens, the red admiral is that most frequently to be seen. They do not appear until later in the year, usually about August, when they may be spotted sucking up the nectar of buddleia, or sweet juices of over-ripe fruits.

Apart from butterflies, many moths may be seen both in the garden and in the house. Among these are the largest of our moths, the hawkmoths. These include the privet hawkmoth which has blackish brown front wings and rear ones striped with pink. These moths can be up to 12cm across and sometimes rest on garden fences. As their name suggests, the caterpillars feed on privet. They are fairly common in Surrey.

Two pinkish coloured hawkmoths, the small elephant hawkmoth and the elephant hawkmoth, may be seen around Surrey dwellings. The former is yellow and pink, the latter green and pink. Sometimes attracted indoors by light, they feed on willowherbs, some of which grow on wasteland, others in the garden. Both species are common.

A range of other moths appear indoors if the window is left open on a warm, summer evening. Many of these are drab and hard to identify, but others are quite distinctive. Of the yellow species, the swallowtail is frequently encountered. On the wing in July, this pale yellow moth has projecting 'tails' on its hindwings. The brownish caterpillar feeds on ivy, hawthorn, elder and blackthorn.

Another yellow moth, but of a far deeper shade, is the brimstone. Far smaller than its butterfly namesake, it has reddish marks on the forewings. The caterpillar feeds on much the same plants as the swallowtail (except ivy). Early specimens of this moth, on the wing in April, arise from overwintering pupae, but brimstones can be seen as late as October.

Feeding on a variety of tree species are the caterpillars of lackey moths, a common species in Surrey. The caterpillars are normally found in colonies, rather like those of peacock butterflies. The adult moths vary in colour from pale ochre yellow to dark brown, but are rarely seen except when attracted indoors by light.

A common and variable species is the heart and dart moth, named after the markings on its wings. It is particularly suited to gardens, feeding on a variety of plants like chickweed, plantain, lettuce and turnips.

Flying in May and June and again in the autumn is the interestingly named setaceous hebrew character. The caterpillar of this species feeds on plants like dock, chickweed and groundsel, all well known garden weeds.

Numerous other moths may be discovered both in and out of the house, of a tremendous variety, from the rather drab vapourer to the colourful large yellow underwing.

On warm nights a number of other insects will come inside. These include craneflies and small flies, gnats and midges. A large proportion of the smaller flies are gall midges – those species which develop inside swollen plant tissues known as galls. Other tiny insects can appear indoors even in mid-winter. The commonest of these winter gnats is known as *Trichocera annulata*. Like most other species of this group, its larvae live mainly among decaying leaves.

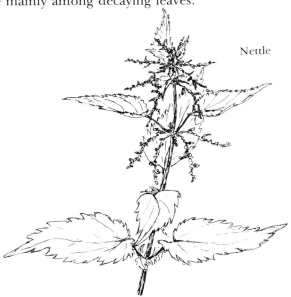

Nettle

Many of the smaller insects of Surrey gardens are far from popular with gardeners. In particular, this applies to the various greenfly and blackfly. An ally against these pests, which suck the juices from plants, are the ladybirds. These are ferocious carnivores, consuming large quantities of aphids. Ladybirds come in a number of varieties, not all of which are red with black spots. The commonest, which is so-coloured, is the seven spot ladybird. The smaller two spot species is also common as is the 22-spot variety. The 22 spot is one of the yellow species and has large numbers (not necessarily 22) of black spots.

Also of value are bees. The first are to be seen early in the season, along with the first flowers. Others are on the wing until late autumn, until the last ivy has flowered. Although both sexes visit the flowers, only the females actively gather pollen and nectar with which to rear their young. Some species have special 'pollen baskets' on their legs into which pollen collected on the rest of the body is stored for the flight back to the nest. In some cases, a bee can carry up to half its own weight in pollen.

Honey bees are among the earliest bees to emerge, to be followed by members of the genus *Andrena*, which nest in the ground and are known as miner bees. All this group are solitary insects, unlike the sociable, hairy, bumble bees. Those seen early in the season have spent the winter hibernating. When nesting, they usually choose a hole either at or below ground level, frequently making use of an old mouse or vole nest.

A number of bumble bees can be recognised. One of our largest species, *Bombus terrestris*, is generally abundant in the county and sports an orange tail. *Bombus lucorum* has much brighter yellow bands on its body and a white tail, whilst *Bombus lapidarius* has a bright red tail and black body.

Wasps come in two main groups – diggers and true wasps. Diggers are all solitary insects, some not particularly wasp-like in appearance. They generally (in gardens) nest in dead wood, drilling neat holes in things like fence posts. True wasps can be either solitary or social. Among these are species which nest in vertical banks and old mortar. Social true wasps are the form most familiar to us, as they build paper nests and fly around sweet substances at tea-time. Other groups of garden insects make use of the warning coloration, even though they possess no sting. Among these are hoverflies.

A wide range of beetles may be encountered in Surrey gardens in addition to ladybirds. The stag beetle is an insect fairly local in its distribution. It has become rarer in the general countryside due to the felling of woodland, in the trees of which its larvae tunnelled. In suburban areas it often makes do with fence timber. The spectacular male, which bears enormous overgrown jaws with which it fights over females, may sometimes be seen flying in early evening, though nothing like as frequently as the cockchafer.

Cockchafers are colourful large beetles, sporting long, feathery orange antennae. On the wing in May and June, these bumbling insects sometimes cause alarm by crashing repeatedly into windows. They are also unpopular with gardeners as their larvae spend several years below ground before maturing, nibbling at the roots of a number of plants. When mature, the adults, if present in large enough numbers, can defoliate trees.

Far more primitive than beetles are the silverfish, which may be disturbed in the kitchen after dark, by putting the light on. A totally wingless insect, the silverfish lives in dark corners, feeding on starch. Covered in silver scales, it does little extensive damage, unless present in enormous numbers, but will nibble bulbs, paper, glue and spilt food in cupboards. Throughout its entire evolution, it is thought never to have developed wings.

Insects are not the only invertebrates to be found living with Man. Woodlice, a group of crustaceans, can often be found both indoors and out. Preferring dark, damp places, woodlice will be discovered under logs and stones in gardens, or dark corners in the house. A number of species may be noted, 42 having been recorded in Britain, although only 29 are thought to be native.

Centipedes and millipedes, despite first appearances, are not closely related. The former normally have one pair of legs on each segment, whereas millipedes have two on most segments. Besides this, there are various other differences. Centipedes will be encountered in a range of habitats including the soil, under stones, in sheds, greenhouses and sometimes indoors. Different species specialise in the main habitat types. To a certain extent, millipedes may be encountered in similar situations, such as compost heaps, under logs, stones, seed trays and so on. Millipedes lay eggs throughout the summer, some simply depositing them in the soil. Many, however, give them some form of protection, such as covering them with saliva, soil, excrement, dead leaves, etc.

Snails are not only food to some thrushes but also provide food to other creatures like hedgehogs, frogs and shrews. Night-time or damp weather is the best time to observe them as they take advantage of such conditions to avoid drying out – their skins are not waterproof. The number of snails present is also controlled by the need for calcium to build their shells. Those of us living on the Downs, therefore, have the greatest variety of snails. However, most places play host to the garden snail, a largely dull, brown creature. In daylight, garden snails often huddle toether under cover of a plant pot, emerging at night to do damage to low-growing fruits and vegetables. They seem to have a homing instinct, returning day after day to the same shelter.

Far less popular than snails are slugs, which are abundant in the garden. Several species may be seen, all of which, to a certain extent, feed on plants. However, their preference is for decaying leaves, so they probably do less harm than they get blamed for. Like snails, they are more often seen in wet weather as they too need to keep damp – they are nothing more than snails without shells. Some species, like *Testacella haliotides* do have tiny shells at the end of their bodies.

Of the completely shell-less species, the one most frequently seen in Surrey gardens will probably be the great grey slug. They thrive around human habitations, even coming inside cellars and damp buildings. Most of their food comprises fungi. Even more common, especially in the vegetable patch, is the fawn and white netted slug.

Among the invertebrates spiders are important, whilst toads and frogs form an interesting part of the vertebrate fauna.

Of those which build a web, the garden spider is one of the commonest. It has a cross-shaped pattern of white dots on its abdomen and is responsible for the beautiful orb webs which sparkle in the sunlight of an autumn morning. Other spiders live in tunnel webs on walls, run along the ground after prey (wolf-spiders), live in flowers often taking on the colour of the flower for camouflage (crab spiders), or stalk their prey, making a sudden leap onto it when close enough (jumping spiders). This last group includes the well-known zebra spider.

Spiders of the *Tegenaria* genus are able to survive long periods without food or water, often in dry situations. Hence their frequency in houses. Among the largest of this group is *Tegeneria gigantea* which is common in Surrey and responsible for the many scares when a large spider hurries across the floor at night. Found in sheds and out-houses is the even longer-legged *Pholcus phalangoides* which makes large, tangled webs. Their legs are about five times the size of their 10mm long body.

Gardens and houses are important for wildlife, but so are many roads. Most of the weeds of gardens are also found on roadsides, where the ground has been disturbed – species like groundsel, broad-leaved dock, ground elder, creeping buttercup and so on. However, many roads have developed a more traditional grassland flora, with flowers like ox-eye daisy, meadow buttercup and many vetches. Plants of disturbed soil may also appear in profusion – for instance poppies along the A246 between West Horsley and Merrow, when it was dualled a few years ago.

Many other species may be seen along roadsides – in fact, a whole range of grassland, hedgerow and woodland species. In May, the lanes of Surrey are dominated by cow parsley, which, in many places, is later replaced by red campion. Where there are ditches, especially

Bramble

wet ones, lady's smock is also prominent, as is the case in the Ockley area.

Before public spending became restricted, there was a constant battle with the Highways Authorities to prevent mowing of verges several times a year. In some cases, even herbicides were applied. Now, cutting is usually performed in a way more beneficial to wildlife, normally not more than once a year. Preferably, this should be done later in the summer, once the plants have had time to flower and set seed. If the verges are not cut at all, we begin to see natural succession taking place. The grasses and flowers become shaded out by shrubs and much of the interest is lost.

One of the biggest nature reserves in Britain is the network of motorways. Generally, the verges are wide and untouched as people are prevented from walking along them. Many Surrey motorways have had little time to develop, only the Reigate to Godstone section of the M25 being fairly long established. In some cases there is the potential for interesting flora to develop, such as where a chalk 'escarpment' has been created across the claylands near Leatherhead.

Roadside hedges present similar opportunities and problems for conservation, as do grasslands. Many landowners do not bother to cut their hedges back as they encroach on the road, necessitating cutting by the local authorities. The cheapest way of doing this uses a flail mounted on the back of a tractor. Although this severely mangles the hedge when done, the hedge usually recovers, leaving little in the way of scars next season. Sometimes, however, hedges have been cut in spring when they are being used for nesting. This is often simply because the amount of cutting necessary across the county as a whole is too much to accomplish outside the nesting season.

Many species of plant and animal can survive in the most inhospitable of conditions. Towns, even country ones like Dorking would, at first glance, appear to offer little opportunity for wildlife. However, in 1985, as part of a Surrey Wildlife Trust 'Out and About' week, a range of activities were organised, which included an afternoon walk around the streets and car parks of Dorking. In just two hours, over 100 species of plants and birds were identified and many others passed over due to lack of time.

Some of the species seen on such a walk were familiar to anyone: daisies growing at the edge of a car park, ragwort in a crack in some concrete steps and ivy trailing around some railings. Others were a little more obscure, like buddleia growing out of the gutter of a shop, male ferns thriving in the shade between two warehouses, or sand martins in the banks around a car park.

Churchyards have several features which make them of benefit to wildlife. Unless the grass is regularly mown, they usually resemble meadows, full of wildflowers and insects. The grassland is rarely disturbed, except to admit a new burial. In addition, the stones themselves support a rich variety of life, including numerous lichens, mosses and a few flowering plants. Many tiny creatures can also be seen, such as red mites, which hurry over the stones.

Wherever Man goes he alters the environment. In Surrey, built-up areas are quite extensive, yet many forms of wildlife have adapted. To conserve our rich heritage of wildlife it is essential that the expansion of built-up land is limited, but we must not forget the wildlife these areas contain. Wildlife should be allowed to thrive in towns, not just for its own benefit, but for ours too.

An old cave at Moor Park, Farnham, provides an ideal roost for several species of bat. (KB)

ABOVE: Lawn left unmown for benefit of wildflowers. BELOW: Sunken
lane in greensand of central Surrey, Friday Street. (KB)

ABOVE LEFT: Nettle, common plant of wasteland. RIGHT: Daisy – a plant which survives in trampled areas due to low habit. BELOW LEFT: Another hedgerow plant – greater stitchwort. RIGHT: Red campion, a common hedgerow flower.

ABOVE: Walls provide a habitat for many plants. BELOW: Well
vegetated car park fringe – home to over 20 plant species.

LEFT: Rhododendron – an unwelcome introduction by Man. RIGHT: Even wasteland can support a range of wildlife. BELOW: Many plants, especially those with windborn seeds, find a home along railway embankments.

ABOVE: Well wooded surburban road, with many bird nesting sites.
BELOW: Acid and alkaline gravestones support different lichens, Mickleham.

ABOVE: Close up of lichens on alkaline gravestone. BELOW: Unmown graveyards are excellent for grassland flowers, Mickleham.

Tomorrow is Too Late

Throughout this book we have explored the diverse range of flora and fauna to be found in this county. The species mentioned form only a small part of those present, the total number of which would take many lifetimes to study. Despite this tremendous variety, much has been lost and will continue to be lost, in the Surrey countryside.

This variety is largely due to the underlying geology, but has also much to do with Man. By clearing the woods, creating fields and heathlands, making ponds and so on, Man has inadvertently benefitted wildlife. Similarly, by building houses and roads, extracting minerals and intensifying agriculture, he has destroyed much.

Perhaps Surrey has suffered most as a result of the growth of London. We have seen that some species, like cowslip were once far more widespread, growing close to what is now central London. Although the Surrey Wildlife Trust continues to operate in the outer London boroughs, much of that part of the county's territory was lost around a century ago, with the creation of the then London County Council. In 1965, the reorganisation of London government saw many parts of the county absorbed into the new boroughs and Greater London. The Greater London Council may now have gone, but the boroughs remain, extending long fingers south towards Redhill and Leatherhead.

Whatever the administrative boundaries, it is the physical ones which have most influenced wildlife. Almost continuous development extends from London to within the county boundaries, to places like Walton-on-Thames, Chessington, Leatherhead, Tadworth, Coulsdon and Caterham. In places, open space, sometimes extensive in area, may be found within the built-up area. In some localities open space has effectively separated Surrey towns from London, but even here the countryside has been degraded due to its closeness to urban land. For example, some farmland, woodland and common keep Chessington from spreading towards Leatherhead. In practice, only the common is truly rural, the farms relying much on selling produce to passing traffic, and Chessington Zoo taking up the rest of the space. Although Leatherhead may have preserved its country town status to the north, it is almost entirely linked to the urban sprawl *via* Epsom and Ashtead in the east.

In 1930 it looked as if Dorking would soon be reached by that same urban sprawl. Surrey County Council learned in that year of the possibility of Norbury Park, covering some 520 hectares in the Mole Valley, being acquired for speculative development. It was realised that the powers held by the various town planning authorities were inadequate to prevent development, so more drastic action was needed. Until the Surrey County Council Act of 1931 gave approval for the purchase of the land, a council member entered into a contract, giving the County Council an option to purchase.

Before the Surrey County Council Act, land could be acquired under the Open Spaces Act, 1906, but had to be used entirely as a public open space. The 1931 Act permitted other activities, such as farming, to be continued on all or part of the area. So Norbury Park became the County's first open space. Today, these areas cover several thousand hectares, ranging in size from tiny, one hectare sites like Betchworth Clump, to the massive 580 hectares of Chobham Common.

Long before the Surrey County Council took steps to protect Norbury Park, the City of London had recognised the need to keep open spaces around the capital. From the 1870s, the Corporation began to acquire land like Farthing Down, Riddlesdown, or Coulsdon Common. Even today, these survive as important wildlife and recreation areas.

The idea of Green Belts, one of which today covers a large proportion of Surrey, is even older. In various forms, they may be traced back to Elizabethan times. Over the years, ideas were modified until, in the inter-war years, the Government set up the Royal Commission on the Distribution of Industrial Population.

The Commission was intended to examine the imbalance that had developed between the south-east, where industries were more modern, unemployment lower and people more prosperous, and the rest of the country. The Commission took its brief further than this, concluding that industry needed more equal distribution throughout the country and that controls were needed on development in the south-east. Similar problems and conclusions can still be identified today.

The Greater London Plan envisaged the Green Belt as four concentric zones. The inner two would comprise the built-up area of London, which would be surrounded by the third, Green Belt zone, stretching some 16km beyond the built-up area. Beyond this, the Outer Country Ring would take overspill new development.

The early success of the Green Belt in Surrey is due largely to the co-operation between Lord Morrison of Lambeth at the London County Council and Lord Chuter Ede, Vice Chairman (and later Chairman) of Surrey County Council. Under the scheme the London County Council (and later the Greater London Council) contributed towards the purchase of land by Surrey local authorities. Other sites were bought without aid from London, whilst some were given to the County.

Following the success of the Green Belt, some councils sought permission to extend the areas covered within their own county. An extension approved in 1973 ensured that almost all of Surrey was within the Green Belt. A few areas have since been excluded, where boundaries have been drawn around towns and villages, to allow for future essential development.

Although the Green Belt was essentially developed to halt the outward expansion of the capital, it is now seen as a method of restricting development within the county. Almost every time a planning application is filed, someone objects that it is against Green Belt policy. However, it is the major developments, such as the M25, which threaten the scheme, and not individual extensions to houses.

Over the years many other bodies have come to own tracts of countryside in Surrey. In particular, one of the largest landowners is the National Trust, which owns over 3,000 hectares, including many important wildlife sites like Box Hill, Frensham Common and Bookham Common.

The public has free access to most National Trust land, which is generally managed for its benefit. However, most properties are also managed in sympathy with wildlife. This trend has become more evident in recent years and is now an essential requirement where National Trust property is scheduled as a Site of Special Scientific Interest. At some properties, information centres have been opened which explain the ecology, as well as the history, of an area. Nature trails have also been marked out, introducing the public to the wealth of wildlife.

At times, conservation can go hand in hand with amenity. Such an example can be found at Leith Hill, where trees felled to improve the view also removed them from the heathland which they were invading. In many cases, however, opening land to the public can have a detrimental effect on its ecology. Scars and erosion gulleys have developed at places like Frensham Common and Box Hill, due to excess pressure. Similar popularity has led to urgent anti-erosion measures around Frensham Great Pond, which was rapidly developing into a sandy beach, devoid of plant life, until areas were fenced off to be revegetated.

Fencing is also necessary where sheep are grazed. Although early grazing experiments made use of temporary fencing, it has been found essential to install permanent fencing where grazing is a regular feature of management. Although this limits access, the National Trust has erected regular stiles. Of course, sheep worrying by dogs is a possible problem in these areas, but has not proved too serious. Heathlands such as Headley Heath would also benefit from selective grazing, but the reaction of local dog walkers has yet to be gauged.

Some properties of the National Trust and other bodies suffer from fires, whether started accidentally or deliberately. Unless part of a management plan, fires are likely to do considerable damage to the ecology of an area, as they are generally uncontrolled. On heathlands they may destroy heathers of varying ages, causing their replacement with even-aged stands. More likely, they will provide ideal conditions for colonising species such as bracken and birch. Where trees have already become established fires occasionally benefit the area by clearing, at least temporarily. This does produce other problems. After the 1976 fires at Thursley, the dead trees took several years to clear. Had they been left, they would have prevented access to vast areas of heath by emergency vehicles during any future fire. The temperature of any such burn would also have been considerably increased.

Whereas the National Trust is usually seen as a body which conserves the countryside, the Forestry Commission is frequently accused of the opposite. Although it owns around one thousand hectares in Surrey, not all of this is coniferous. Much of this land is open to the public, either solely on rights of way or, in many cases, on all tracks within the property. Whilst the variety of life may be less than that found in semi-natural woodlands, even conifer plantations provide homes for some birds and mammals such as roe deer. Many of the smaller copses once owned by the Commission, but never planted with exotic species, have been sold in recent years, at Government insistence. This has left the Commission largely with the more economical, but less interesting plantations.

In 1949, the National Parks and Access to the Countryside Act made provision for setting up the Nature Conservancy (Council), National Nature Reserves and Local Nature Reserves.

Local Nature Reserves are owned by the local authority and are governed by by-laws. In Surrey, such reserves have been set up at Chobham Common, Hackhurst Down, Nore Hill Pinnacle and Staffhurst Wood under the ownership of the County Council. Additionally, two reserves are managed under this scheme by Waverley Borough Council. Although the responsibility of the respective authorities, consultation is maintained with the Nature Conservancy Council and other bodies.

National Nature Reserves come under the direct control of the Nature Conservancy Council. Surrey has only one, the internationally important Thursley reserve.

The Nature Conservancy Council are also responsible for notifying Sites of Special Scientific Interest. Under the Wildlife and Countryside Act 1981, these have to be renotified even if previously declared. As the name suggests, these are sites of particular interest for their wildlife, usually among the best of their type in the county. The owners of such sites are provided with a map, details of why the site is of value and a list of damaging operations which must not be carried out without prior consultation with the Nature Conservancy Council. This renotification process has put a considerable burden on the NCC, so there is a backlog of sites.

The late 1950s saw a tremendous interest in the countryside. Following the war, changes had become more rapid as the nation sought to regain prosperity. By 1959, people were aware that much of our heritage would be lost should nothing be done. During that year, two organisations were formed which have done much to prevent this happening in Surrey.

One, the Conservation Corps, first met on Box Hill. It was formed to carry out practical work in the countryside with the aim of improving it for both wildlife and people. Its first job was to clear scrub from the famous chalk slopes, thereby allowing the re-establishment of the grassland and its rich flora. Some people saw the group as vandals, destroying what had developed naturally over a number of years. As time went by, others realised the importance of managing the countryside and joined in. Today, the organisation is known as the British Trust for Conservation Volunteers. It has established a nationwide network of offices, staff and associated local groups, carrying out thousands of man-days' work annually.

The other society founded in 1959 was the Surrey Naturalists' Trust. A group of naturalists (John Clegg, John Sankey and Cyril Diver) exchanged letters about forming a county trust. Other naturalists, well known in Surrey, also became involved in the early days – people such as Ted Lousley and Oleg Polunin. The actual birth of the Trust took place in Kingston on 31 March 1959 and it was incorporated as a limited company just before Christmas that same year.

An early activity was to establish a network of local contacts across the county, who could keep an eye on developments in their areas and encourage other people to join. Another was the leasing of the Trust's first reserve at Seale Chalk Pit, below the Hog's Back.

During the 1960s, there were a number of achievements. Early in its existence, the Trust negotiated with the War Department over the use of Surrey commons for military training. This led to reassurances that no further deterioration would be allowed.

Another was the steady stream of new reserves. Vann Lake was established under an agreement in 1964. In 1965 Bay Pond at Godstone became the Trust's first owned property, when it was donated. Excellent chalk grassland reserves, namely Headley Warren and Dawcombe, followed later in the decade.

Also in the sixties came innovation – the nature trail. Intended to encourage both children and adults to take a greater interest in the countryside, by showing them just how much could be seen in a relatively short walk, nature trails quickly caught on throughout the country. Today, they are a familiar feature of the countryside. Their great advantage is their simplicity. All that is needed is a marked path, a selection of numbered stopping points and a descriptive leaflet.

Most of the Surrey Naturalists' Trust trails were set up for a week, during which time several thousand visitors, including a high proportion of schoolchildren, paid a visit. From an educational view point, this was better than nothing, but in no way catered for the special needs of individual schools or pupils.

In 1971, Nower Wood near Leatherhead came on the market. Adjoining the existing Headley Warren reserve, Nower Wood covered 32 hectares, including a range of different woodland types and five ponds. The Trust decided to purchase the wood and develop, not only a nature reserve, but the first educational reserve. Woodland is by far the best habitat in which to do this, because it is far more resistant to trampling.

Buildings were erected to form a centre and classroom and, under the guidance of a teacher-warden, Nower Wood became a model for similar centres throughout the country. Each visiting school is booked in for a day or half-day, and courses are tailored to their exact requirements. Many come back year after year, but need to book early, as the centre is generally full a year in advance.

As a further mark of the respect in which the Trust was held within the county, it was asked to prepare a survey of all the county's natural habitats, to be included in the information upon which

Surrey downland butterflies: ABOVE LEFT: chalkhill blue; RIGHT; silver-
spotted skipper; CENTRE LEFT: small blue; RIGHT: Duke of Burgundy;
BELOW LEFT: brown argus; RIGHT: dingy skipper.

PLATE VII

Surrey moths: ABOVE LEFT: speckled yellow and RIGHT: alder dagger-
moth. CENTRE LEFT: Forester moth and RIGHT: six-spot burnet.
BELOW LEFT: Emperor moth and RIGHT: bee hawk.

PLATE VIII

the Surrey Structure Plan was to be based. Adopting a system previously used by the Nature Conservancy Council to survey West Sussex, the survey results were presented to the County Council in the form of two maps. One evaluated numerically the habitat value of each of the 1,700 one-kilometre squares in the county. The other showed sites of high natural habitat value, ignoring the 1km squares. Data collection was based on aerial photographs provided by the Council, with as much ground checking as possible.

The great value of this project was not just the input it allowed into the county structure plan, but the data it provided for the Trust about its own county. Additionally, it showed how ordinary

Coppice woodland

members could participate in relatively simple survey work, which would be of great conservation value.

The Trust continued to acquire reserves until, in 1976, it managed fourteen. Most of these were managed under agreement with the owners, but one new reserve, Wallis Wood, was donated in 1974. In the south of the county, close to the Sussex border, this 13 hectare wood was an old hazel coppice with largely oak standards. The coppicing cycle was not too far gone to be quickly restored, enabling the Trust to own a reserve where constant annual management would show lasting results.

113

Early in 1976, the Surrey Naturalists' Trust members voted to change the name of the organisation to Surrey Trust for Nature Conservation. The old name was often confused with the National Trust, an equally worthy, but totally separate organisation. Furthermore, the name also implied that members needed to be expert naturalists, rather than emphasising the true role the organisation played in the conservation of the flora and fauna of the county.

Undoubtedly, the most important reserve with which the Trust had been associated was that at Thursley. Recognised by the Nature Conservancy Council as a Grade 1 Site of Special Scientific Interest, the reserve was managed in cooperation with Colonel Whitbread as a Trust reserve. The greatest expense involved was the full-time warden, although Colonel Whitbread contributed his share. Financial pressure on the Trust forced it to approach the Nature Conservancy Council for a grant in 1974, but this was refused on the grounds that it was a recurring expense, for which grants were not designed.

After spending some time negotiating for a lease, the Nature Conservancy Council acted quickly when, in 1977, Colonel Whitbread put his estate on the market. Successfully completing the purchase in 1978, the NCC then entered into an agreement with the Surrey Trust for Nature Conservation to continue day-to-day management on its behalf. After several years, the total management of Thursley passed to the Nature Conservancy Council, whose resources were better suited to such an important site.

The workload on the Trust's full time paid staff continued to grow throughout the 1970s. By 1984, it was realised that there was greater potential for increasing membership, funding and public awareness of the Trust than could be exploited by the existing network of volunteer helpers.

The decision was taken to appoint a Development Officer, on the basis of a reducing grant for the first three years from the Nature Conservancy Council; with the aid of a Development Committee plans were drawn up for a major membership campaign and appeal in 1986, in accordance with an organisational plan produced in 1985. It was also decided to once again change the name of the organisation to the Surrey Wildlife Trust.

The need for a greater public awareness of conservation in the county is evidenced by a repeat of the 1974/5 survey for the Surrey Structure Plan, in 1984/5.

Analysis of the results have shown that, over the ten year period, 7,200 hectares of Surrey have been affected by change in some way. Almost 4,000 hectares have suffered loss of important wildlife habitat. In addition, 217km of hedgerows have been lost.

Although precise figures were not always available for the areas of different habitats present in 1975, estimates can be made. From these it is clear that some 7% of woodland, 16% of heathland and 25% unimproved grassland have been lost over the succeeding ten years.

Not all change has been for the worse. Some 1,830 hectares of high value habitat has been gained over the same period. However, as is usual in conservation, new areas of habitat take some time to develop as rich associations of wildlife, as those which have existed for several hundred years.

Over the county as a whole, 40% of the habitat change has occurred as a result of agriculture. Farming is also, not suprisingly, responsible for 92% of the hedgerow loss. Whilst this may be construed as over-management, it must also be borne in mind that 22% of loss is due to 'natural causes' – otherwise known as neglect. This includes the loss of downland and heathland to scrub, as well as many other changes.

Forestry, still not a particularly important influence in Surrey, is responsible for just 14% of change. Even housing, roads, minerals and industrial development together caused only 19% of habitat loss.

What these figures illustrate is that, for the county as a whole, only about one-quarter of the habitat losses are due to activities for which planning permission is required. The major proportion require no formalities at all.

Improvements in data collection also show where losses may be expected in the future, due to neglect. 22% of the remaining heathland in Surrey, for example, is more than 50% covered in trees and shrubs – formidable management problem.

Several conclusions can be drawn. Firstly, it is the rarer habitats, such as heathland and grassland, which are suffering a disproportionate loss. Secondly, it is those changes for which there are least controls that are having the greatest impact. Thirdly, without a strategy to protect vulnerable areas currently outside planning control, much of our wildlife not already protected by conservation bodies will be lost. Any strategy which may be developed must allow for local variation. For example, the main cause of habitat change in Mole Valley is agriculture, whilst in Spelthorne it is mineral working. Surrey Heath suffers most from natural losses.

It is always difficult to predict the future as the results of past attempts show. However, a few broad assumptions can be made.

Over the past few years, there has been a greater acceptance of advice from bodies like the Surrey Wildlife Trust by local authorities in the county. In a number of cases, this has led to the inclusion of sites of ecological value in local plans. Whilst these do not have any guaranteed protection, their inclusion ensures that conservationists will be consulted over any proposed changes. There seems no reason why a way cannot be found to extend this system to the wider countryside.

Another increasingly obvious fact is the inability of the Common Market to continue to subsidise agricultural production, in excess of demand. Even the National Farmers Union agree that there will be a significant drop in the amount of land needed in production. There are a number of possible uses to which that land could be put.

One is for existing land to be used less intensively. This could be achieved either by reducing the input of fertilizers and pesticides, or by reducing the area of each field actively farmed. A return could be made to just sowing spring crops, rather than winter ones as well. Any of these options would benefit wildlife.

Leaving land fallow between crops would involve regular ploughing of the fallow fields, thereby reducing their value to nature. However, taking whole fields out of production could have great benefits, but only as long as the wildlife which colonises it is actively managed. One possibility is for subsidies to allow the employment of people to actively manage the countryside on a large scale.

If adequate financial incentives can be provided, much farmland could be used to plant trees. Whilst some broadleaves would be beneficial it is likely for financial reasons, that most planting would be coniferous or, at best, mixed. Even so, this would probably be more beneficial to wildlife than the present agricultural land. What should now end is the destruction of woodland for agriculture but, until farmland becomes available to forestry, we can expect more conversion of native woodlands to conifers.

Over the last thirty years, there has been a tremendous increase in public awareness of the importance of conservation. Even so, that reaction has resulted in only minimal conservation on the ground. The changes which are now almost upon us provide an excellent opportunity to alter Surrey for the better and reverse centuries of loss. If this is to happen, everyone in Surrey will need to do something. If we leave it to someone else, our nature reserves will be like museums in a sterile countryside, and the subject of this book will become nothing more than history. Action is needed now. Tomorrow is too late.

ABOVE: Gravel workings – a common sight in some parts of the county. They can be restored. (KB) LEFT: Long distance footpaths provide opportunities to watch wildlife, but RIGHT: even horseriding can cause erosion, in excess.

ABOVE: Public pressure v conservation: Frensham Great pond on a Sunday. BELOW: Restoring a village pond with the help of the local community.

ABOVE: Conservation volunteers clearing scrub, and BELOW: a
recently created pond at Headley Heath

118

Appendix I: Wildlife Sites in Surrey

The following gazetteer includes a selection of the best wildlife sites in Surrey, together with their main wildlife interest. Many are open to the public, although some have restricted access. Details of Surrey Wildlife Trust reserves and access arangements may be obtained from SWT, Hatchlands, East Clandon, Guildford, Surrey.

Key

LNR	Local Nature Reserve	R	Access restricted to certain paths or times
MVDC	Mole Valley District Council	RSPB	Royal Society for the Protection of Birds
NCC	Nature Conservancy Council	SCC	Surrey County Council
NNR	National Nature Reserve	SP	Special permit required
NT	National Trust	SWT	Surrey Wildlife Trust
O	Open	WBC	Waverley Borough Council
P	Privately owned		

NATURE RESERVES

Name	Map ref.	Access
ALDERS, ELSTEAD (SWT)	SU915437	SP
Wet woodland and ponds in old quarry		
BAGMOOR COMMON (SWT)	SU926423	O
Mixed woodland, good for butterflies		
BARFOLD COPSE (RSPB)	SU925325	O
Mixed woodland, typical woodland birds		
BAY POND (SWT)	TQ351515	R
Lake, reed beds, alder swamp and farmland. Lake visible from footpath		
CHOBHAM COMMON (SCC/LNR)	SU975655	O
Excellent heath and bog with some woodland		
CUCKNELLS WOOD (SWT)	TQ041430	R/SP
Mixed woodland on sandstone/clay spring line		
GODSTONE RESERVOIRS (SWT)	TQ357519	SP
Two reservoirs in old sand workings. Over 100 bird species		
GRACIOUS POND (SWT)	SU987638	SP
Wet and dry mixed woodland on site of old lake		
GRAEME HENDREY WOOD (SWT)	TQ346501	R
Deciduous wood in old sandstone quarry. Good for ferns and mosses		
HACKHURST DOWN (SCC & NT/LNR)	TQ093486	O
Chalk downland, excellent for flowers. Colony of juniper		
HEADLEY WARREN (SWT)	TQ194545	SP
Chalk grassland and woods, excellent for lepidoptera		
MOOR PARK (SWT)	SU867459	O
Deep alder swamp visible from footpath and boardwalk		
NOWER WOOD (SWT)	TQ193546	R
Mixed woodland with four ponds. Educational reserve		
SEALE CHALK PIT (SWT)	SU899482	SP
Chalk quarry with typical downland flora and fauna		
STAFFHURST WOOD (SCC/LNR)	TQ413485	O
Good example of Wealden woodland on clay		
THUNDRY MEADOWS (SWT)	SU896440	O
Unimproved wet and dry meadows, alder carr, farmland, ditches, riverbank		
THURSLEY COMMON (NCC/NNR)	SU898410	O
Wet and dry heathland, woodland, bog, ponds. Excellent for dragonflies		
VANN LAKE (SWT)	TQ157394	R
Eight acre lake and surrounding woodland in steep valley		
WALLIS WOOD (SWT)	TQ121388	O
Coppiced woodland and pasture. Best in spring for flowers		

Name	*Map ref.*	*Access*
ASHTEAD COMMON (P)	TQ175597	O
Grassy common on clay with ancient oak trees		
ASHTEAD PARK (MVDC)	TQ192585	O
Parkland with two lakes, hornbeam trees and wild flowers		
BANSTEAD DOWNS	TQ252612	O
Downland on borders of London		
BANSTEAD WOODS/FAMES ROUGH	TQ265580	O
Mixed woodland and chalk grassland with many unusual plants		
BARN ELMS RESERVOIRS	TQ229770	SP
Good birdwatching site. Permits from Thames Water Authority		
BOOKHAM COMMON (NT)	TQ128565	O
Woodland, grassland, ponds and ditches. Probably the best documented site in the country due to work by London Natural History Society		
BOX HILL (NT)	TQ180515	O
Very important chalk grassland and woodland site		
DEVILSDEN WOODS	TQ304570	O
Woodland and downland near Croydon		
EPSOM COMMON	TQ190605	O
Grassy common with two lakes, adjoining Ashtead Common		
FRENSHAM COMMON (WBC/NT)	SU850405	O
Heathland, pinewoods and two extensive lakes. Best avoided summer Sunday's		
GATTON PARK (NT/P)	TQ265525	O/SP
Woodlands (open) and large lake with heronry (private)		
HEADLEY HEATH (NT)	TQ200535	O
Heathland on North Downs ridge, with ponds and birch woodland		
HINDHEAD (NT)	SU895360	O
Extensive series of heath, wood and common at high altitude		
HOLMWOOD COMMON (NT)	TQ175456	O
Wet wooded common on clay, with several ponds		
LEITH HILL (NT)	TQ135430	O
High woodland and heath on greensand with bilberry		
MERROW DOWNS	TQ035497	O
Chalk grassland and scrub		
NEWLANDS CORNER (SCC)	TQ040495	O
Chalk grassland and scrub with Silent Pool in valley below		
PARK DOWNS	TQ270585	O
Chalk grassland and scrub with many warblers		
QUEEN ELIZABETH II RESERVOIR	TQ120670	SP
Excellent bird watching site, especially in winter		
RANMORE COMMON (NT)	TQ140510	O
Wooded common with a variety of birds, including hawfinches. Also, Denbies, chalk downland		
REIGATE HEATH	TQ237503	O
Heath and woodland, but partly a golf course		
RICHMOND PARK	TQ200730	O
Massive Royal Park, including grassland, woods, ponds and deer		
SELSDON WOOD	TQ365615	R
Good for woodland birds on edge of Croydon		
SHEEPLEAS (SCC)	TQ086515	O
Chalk grassland and woods, excellent for flowers		
STAINES MOOR	TQ033730	O
One of the few remaining unimproved grasslands on the Thames gravels		
STAINES RESERVOIR	TQ050730	O
Good bird watching from central causeway		
WIMBLEDON COMMON	TQ225715	O
Exceptionally diverse common near to London		

Appendix II: References and Further Reading

BRANDON P. (1977) *A History of Surrey*. Phillimore.
BRITISH ASSOCIATION FOR THE ADVANCEMENT OF SCIENCE (1975) *The Surrey Countryside*. University of Surrey.
BRITISH TRUST FOR ORNITHOLOGY (1976) *The Atlas of Breeding Birds in Britain and Ireland*.
BURTON J.A. (1974) *The Naturalist in London*. David and Charles.
CHINERY M. (1977) *The Natural History of the Garden*. Fontana.
DREWETT J. (1985) *Shire County Guide Surrey*. Shire.
FLETCHER JONES P. (1972) *Richmond Park; Portrait of a Royal Playground*. Phillimore.
HAES E.C.M. (1977) *Natural History of Sussex*. Flare.
HEINZEL H., FITTER R., PARSLOW J. (1972) *The Birds of Britain and Europe*. Collins.
JACKSON A.A. (Ed.) (1977) *Ashtead A Village Transformed*. Leatherhead and District Local History Society.
JONES D. (1983) *Spiders of Britain and Northern Europe*. Country Life.
LOUSLEY J.E. (1976) *Flora of Surrey*. David and Charles.
MABEY R. (1974) *The Roadside Wildlife Book*. David and Charles.
MANNING S.A. (1974) *The Naturalist in South-East England*. David and Charles.
MONTIER D. (Ed.) (1977) *Atlas of Breeding Birds of the London Area*. Batsford.
NAIRN I., PEVSNER N. (1971) *The Buildings of England: Surrey*. Penguin.
PARR D. (Ed.) (1972) *Birds in Surrey 1900–1970*. Batsford.
ROSE F. (1981) *The Wild Flower Key*. Warne.
ROYAL SOCIETY FOR THE PROTECTION OF BIRDS (1970) *Farming and Wildlife – A Study in Compromise*. RSPB.
SITWELL N. (1984) *The Shell Guide to Britain's Threatened Wildlife*. Collins.
SOUTH R. (1961) *The Moths of the British Isles*. Warne.
SURREY BIRD CLUB (1965–1984) *Surrey Bird Reports*.
SURREY NATURALISTS' TRUST (1974–1976) *Newsletters 35–41*.
SURREY TRUST FOR NATURE CONSERVATION (1976–1986) *Newsletters 42–72*.
WARREN A. and GOLDSMITH F.B. (Eds.) (1974) *Conservation in Practice*. Wiley.
WOOLDRIDGE S.W. and GOLDRING F. (1953) *The Weald*. Collins.

House sparrows

General Index

Figures in italics refer to illustrations

122

Species Index

124

Subscribers

Presentation Copies

1 Surrey Wildlife Trust
2 Royal Society for Nature Conservation
3 Nature Conservancy Council
4 Surrey County Council
5 National Trust
6 Surrey Biological Record Centre
7 David Bellamy

8 John Drewett
9 Clive & Carolyn Birch
10 Rosalie S. Thompson
11 Andrew Davies
12 Keith Betton
13 Jerry Lockett
14 Ken Wilmott
15 David N. Robinson
16 Brian J. Cooper
17 Peter Langtree
18 D.A. Jackson
19
20 Alan Gifford
21 Robert Smyth
22 Norman E. Goddard
23 Mr & Mrs S.J.
24 Whitten
25 Weybridge Museum
26 B.H. Mackenzie
27 H.H. Percy
28 Andrew Barrett
29 Graham Avison
30 M. Walpole
31 Peter J. White
32 Mrs J. Anderson
33 M.K. Frost
34 Mrs D.L. Brookman
35 Mrs R.E. Scott
36 Edward & Anne Lloyd
37 Peter & Marjorie Julian
38 Dr D.A. Newman
39 Victoria & Albert Museum
40 P.D. Dickin
41 D.A. Coleman
42 Peter J.A. Livesley
43 Margaret F. Birley
44 Mrs Pearl Small
45 Lydia Carter
46 William Bosanquet
47 Beryl Higgins
48 Keith Aspden
49
50 Richard Price
51 Dr D.R. Dance

52 Dr & Mrs F.H. Staines
53 Eric D. Boyland
54 G.E.V. Rochfort RAE
55 Stella White
56 J.G. Miller
57 A.J. Petrie
58 Donovan & Peggy Dawe
59 Janet Spayne
60 Keith Alexander
61 Dr C.B. Wain
62 Mrs E.M. Curtis
63 M.C. Wyatt
64 Dr M.E. Archer
65 Dr David Corke
66 R.G.N. Bird
67 Mr & Mrs R.B. Adamson
68 S.C.A. Holmes
69 Iain John Foster
70 E.A. Crossland
71 D.P.M. Young
72 Ian Tilbury
73 David Page
74 Hilary & Ray Essen
75 Louis Essen
76 Pam Middleton
77 Ronald J. Post
78 E.E. Deeks
79 Claire Entwisle
80 Mrs P.F. Collins
81 Audrey Fry
82 Sally Gray
83 Mary M. Bishop
84 Adrian Davies
85 A. Trubshaw
86 Alison Cane
87 Mrs P.K. Verrall
88 Lawrence R. Harvey
89 Mrs Ann R. Hanson
90 Helen Trim
91 Deborah Craft
92 Robert Tarring
93 Miss M.J. Bettany
94 M. Woolven
95 Bruce Poulter
96 Graham Curtis

97 Wing Commander R.H.B. Forster
98 Miss Wendy Allen
99 David G.E. Knight
100 Mary Goodman
101 R.A. Davis
102 Mr & Mrs P. Edwards
103 Michael Philip Michaels
104 N.A. Callow
105 Janice & Clive Fisher
106 T.F.C. Sankey
107 David Ricketts
108 Miss M.E. Paul
109 Fiona Eldridge & Jane Hawkes
110 Mrs R.L. Cross
111 Mrs E.J.R. Simmonds
112 Sylvia Payne
113 Brian & Bronwen Mills
114 Dr & Mrs B.M. Spooner
115 K.R. Mellen
116
117 B. Dulake
118 Barry Kenneth Hilling
119 C.K. Dunkley
120 Edward W. Petts
121 Jean E.A. Hemens
122 M.L. Burge
123 Miss Joan Bower
124 Keith Barnett
125 V.K. Zietz
126 Miss S.M. Collinson
127 Helen Pool
128 P.J. Holdaway
129 Mrs P. Loarridge
130 Ken J. Willmott
131 G.G. Campbell
132 Mrs Margaret Shipton
133 Eric Mills
134 Monica Hale
135 Peter D. Jones

136 Rupert B.R. Harrison
137 Mr & Mrs E. Lester
138 R.C. Workman
139 Judith M. Christie
140 Gerald Early
141 J.W. Neve
142 Susan Terry
143 D.W. Clarkson Webb
144 A.F. Machiraju
145 Prof Robert C.G. Williams OBE
146 Nigel Coates
147 Dr & Mrs M.O. Moss
148 E.W. Padwick
149 P. Bailey
150 Gaynor Gatty Saunt
151 Miss Nancy B. Williamson
152 Mrs Marjorie Corry
153 D.A. Connell
154 Mrs Jean Graham
155 Mrs Sheila Lermon
156 G.E. John
157 Lesley A.M. Williams
158 Mrs P.G. Turpin
159 Judith M. Nelson
160 N. Wenham
161 Ian Davies
162 Paul J. Krause
163 Ann Walford
164 Clive McDowell
165 David J. Fisher
166 Mrs O.M. Davenport
167 Mrs Gillian H. Stribley
168 C.J. Harmon
169 John W. Edwards
170 Mrs J. Breen
171 Croydon Natural History & Scientific Society Ltd
172 R.T. McAndrew
173 D.E.V. Wilman
174 Ken Hill
175 Dr Geoffrey Beven
176 Susan & Patrick Codd

178	E. Lawrence Bee	236	L.F. Fish
179	Ian Todd	237	Michael Andrews
180	Mrs V. Perkins	238	Mr & Mrs D.S. Corben
181	Patricia Duffy	239	Betty Cutchey
182	L.C. Upsdell	240	Mrs Eve Brooks
183	O.B.J. French	241	David Moss
184	Mrs E.M.F. Catmur	242	D.C. Knight
185	Stephen Berry	243	E.W. Adams
186	J. Kinsman	244	Georgina Carrington
187		245	Diana M. Partridge
188	Miss Barbara Pearce	246	John E. Millard
189	Eric W. Groves	247	John Perkins
190	Derek Brocklebank	248	D.E.W. Southgate
191	R.F.C. Zamboni	249	Miss Mary Swain
192	Sarah Manklow	250	Miss Phyllis Bartlett
193	Joan Slaughter	251	David Edwardson
194	Alan Woolgar	252	Mrs B.E. Money
195	C.W. Plant	253	E.J. Williams
196	Judith Diment	254	Mr & Mrs R.E. Todd
197	R.A. Ledsom	255	Michael Herbert
198	Harry Dumler	256	David W. Walker
199	Patrick & Mary-Clare Sheahan	257	A.W. Dymond
200	Denis Joslin	258	M.N. Clifford
201	Mrs Terri Last	259	Mrs Fiona Mearns
202	Mr & Mrs G. Williams	260 279	Surrey Wildlife Trust
203	George T. Ripley	280	Mrs G.L. Whittle
204	Denis C. Rice	281	D.A. Rossell
205	R.D. Evans	282	Patrick Casey
206	Michael John Cobb	283	Anne Hadley
207	Dr John Watson	284	J.W.A. Cobbett
208	Mrs E.M. Burrell	285	Mrs Barbara Blatchford
209	Joan E. Nettleton Hill	286	Mrs Jean M. Short
210	F. McLaren	287	Andrew Webb
211	Simon G. Powell	288	Joyce Gadsby
212	E.S. Lewis	289	Audrey Podmore
213	Tricia Samuel	290	Dr P. Cureton
214	Roger Tabor	291	Miss Dorothy Gibbs
215	H. John Dickinson	292	H.M.V. Wilsdon
216	Mrs D.M. Gardner	293	Mrs Doreen Harrison
217	Dr A.S. Thorley	294	J.K.M. Sanderson
218	L.G. Green	295	Norman Elliott Shaw
219	F. Nigel Hepper	296	Michael Colin Taylor
220	Ruth M. Post	297	Spelthorne Natural History Society
221	J.W.E. Johnson	298	H.W. Evans
222	Paul A. Sokoloff	299	Alvin Smith
223	Professor W.G. Challoner FRS	300	Sir Norman Statham
224	R.A. Hayes	301	Mrs J.E. Gill
225	Ronald Ditchfield	302	P.C. Holland
226 227	Mrs Mary Jobbins	303	Varlon Beeson
228	Surrey Archaeological Society	304	London Borough of Richmond upon Thames
229 230	Leslie Frank Rodgers	305	
231	Mrs K.R. Edwards	306	J.A. Peacock
232	Lionel George Frusher	307	Jean K. Skinner
233	Miss E.O. Mercer	308	Mrs S. Edge
234	A.J. Down	309	R.F. Bretherton
235	Brian T. Nobbs	310	Audrey Insch
		311	Mr & Mrs R.N. Gutteridge
		312	Philip B. Woodall

313	Dr Simon Archer	372	Clare & Mark Kitchen
314	R.W.A. Craigie	373	M. Boulby
315	Ruth C. Fodor	374	Dr Faith Speller
316	John Cresswell	375	Martin Catt
317	W.T. Jeffery	376	Herbert O. John
318	E.R. Gates	377	Roy Edmunds
319	Charles Peeler	378	J.D.G. Gradidge
320	London Natural History Society	379	Kingston Heritage Service
321	Mrs Brigitte Jennings	380	Martyn Mance
322	Peter Elford	381	Anne Folkes
323	P.J. Maule-Oatway	382	Miss M.W. Power
324	David S. Kirtley	383	David Rolfe
325	R.A. Carpenter	384	Austin Spindler
326	Ms J.A. Stamford	385	D. Manson
327	T.H.P. O'Brien	386	Dr P.G. Botham
328	R.R.C. Johnson	387	Miss B.G. Browning
329	William R. Rogers	388 389	E. Clear
330	R.J. Swindells	390	Thomas A. Skinner
331	Leonard Ennis	391	Randolph Cock
332	Rowland Baker	392	Mrs B. Harwood
333	Lesley & Jim Alloway	393	G.E. Bavin
334	Carole E. Neeser	394	E.S. Tucker
335	Mrs M.B. Knott	395	P.W. Allsopp
336	Richard Sammons	396	Miss W.S. Rodgers
337	Mrs D. Herlihy	397	Dennis D. Dormer
338	Padraig, Mary & Nicholas Herlihy	398	Joan Mary Curtis
339	T.E. Daniels	399	Clive William Martin
340	Colin Nunn	400	Joan Barter
341	P.L. Rabbetts	401	T.T. Jones
342	Dr F.G.C. Meynen	402	Mrs E.C. Baxter
343	Miss S. Webb	403	Graham Cooper
344	E.D. Mercer	404	Miss J.M. Smith
345	Russell Baker	405	H.M. Burkill
346	Leonard Edwards	406	David Hill
347	David Harris	407	Lawrence Smith
348	Margaret Harris	408	Christine King
349	Mrs Hilary Young	409	Mrs Margaret Mitchell
350	G.H. Green	410	Bryan G. Nelson
351	H. Frith	411	Malcolm T. Craymer
352	E.G. Cobb	412	Marjorie Arbury
353	William Wallace	413	Dr J.W. Watson
354	Mrs G. Lejeune	414	P.J.M. Nethercott
355	Dr Robert Woodward	415	David Sewell
356	Jackie Malyon	416	Sandra Evans
357	Dr T. Cavalier-Smith	417	Ralph G. Stephens
358	E. Mary Boothroyd Brooks	418	Mrs Michelle Hoad
359	Elsa E.P. Miller	419	Mrs Paula Marsh
360	Ros Evans	420	Kathryn Whittleton
361	Pamela Chubb	421	Michael David Squires
362	P.M. Washer	422	Leonard G. Cook
363	Miss Ellen Loader	423	A.V. Mascull
364	Mrs E.M. Doncaster MBE	424	Miss J.K. Huish
365	K. Barnett	425	Waverley Borough Council
366	Mrs R.L. Cross	426 427	Mrs I.P. Cann
367	Miss Pamela Hewett	428	J.M. Milner FLS
368	Dr A.J. Ward Smith	429	Elizabeth Wood
369	Arthur Thomas Brinkman	430	Susan Oestel
370	Jennifer J. White		
371	T.M. Hotten		

431 Heloise Collier
432 Miss E.M. Collman
433 A.R.F. Macleod
434 Rose Harrison
435 Stuart H. Chambers
436 R.G. Ackers
437 T. Beaumont
438 Michael & Patricia Cook
439 Mrs J.P. Sivers
440 Miss J.M. Mitchell
441 A. Youngs
442 Dr Geoffrey Robb
443 Jenny Cater
444 Miss Freda Smith
445 Paul Morrison
446 Jon Moore
447 M.J.S. Doran
448 Conservators Epsom & Walton Downs
449 P.C.V. Durell
450 H.W. Mackworth-Praed
451 Mr & Mrs John Bennetts
452 Keith F. Betton
453 Pippa Hyde
454 Thomas George Perkins
455 Miss D.A. Phillips
456 John W. Everett
457 Philip Broadbent-Tale
458 Linda Heath
459 Nicola Penford
460 A.F. Wilson
461 D.G. Potts
462 Mrs B.J.F. Allen
463 R.G. Bishop
464 J.F. Bower
465 Janet M. Hatton
466 Roy R. Guy
467 Derek Williams
468 Faye Norman
469 Mabel G.E. Berry
470 Mrs I.K. Robinson
471 Sayers Croft Rural Centre
472 Ian J. Kenton
473 Jerry Lockett
474 Mary-Rose Murphy
475 Surrey County Council
539
540 Miss Doreen M. Cleland
541 E. Budgen
542 Chris Rose
543 Kenneth Andrews
544
545 Diana M. Hannon
546 Holmesdale Natural History Club
547 Mrs Margaret B. Walker
548 Miss M.E.M. Libbis

549 G.I. Comerford
550
551 Sara Shepley
552 Elizabeth Whitehead
553 K.H. Baker
554 Robert Apsion
555 John Steer
556 C.H. Duvall
557 Rowena Joan Hall
558 Mrs D.B. Redfern
559 Miss D.J.T. Ayres
560 L.J. Collins
561 Mrs Joan Mary Oldroyd
562 Mrs A.L. Lewis
563 Dr A.R. Graham
564 D.W. Hughes
565 Mrs Engeline C. Gape
566 Miss J. de Rochas
567 K.S. Pankhurst
568 Miss W.M. Ariss
569 Mrs Avril Roberts
570 Alix MacAndrews
571 Mrs P.M.I. Hook
572 Captain A.E.T. Christie RN ret
573 Mrs P.D. Prince
574 P.W. Brown
575 Cherry Harborne
576 Peter Bethney
577 C. Sylvia Ker
578 Michael M. Gilmore
579 Oliver Smart
580 D. Morgan Evans
581 Anthony Rampton
582 K.F. & M.C. Bushell
583 Lynn Philpott
584 Peter Andrew Hockham
585 J.S. Downham
586 Graham Roberts
587 Mrs Janet M. Craske
588 Mr & Mrs F. Moorse
589 Dr D. Hetherington
590 Miss Mary Biggart
591 Geoffrey Cuttle
592 Miss Wynne Bartlett
593 Eunice Mary Elliott
594 J.F. Hearnden
595 Miss L. Cowper
596 Jack Rickard
597 John E. Cooter
598 John Mould
599 F.L. Ryan
600 Miss J.M. Foster
601 Mrs P.A. Jameson
602 Stephen & Kate Sankey
603 Mrs M.C. Parslow
604 Anne M. Woods
605 Norman W. Collop
606 Kenneth Bradford
607 Mrs D.F. Andrews

608 Miss J.M. Harries
609 Lady Kahn-Freund
610 K.N. Hardy
611 Peter Slade
612 Dr J.V. & Dr H.S.D. Leonard
613 Eileen Lloyd
614 Patricia Martin
615 J.E. Harvey
616 Barbara Softly
617 John Clegg
618 N.C. Roles
619 J.A. Woodley
620 Peter Jevon
621 D.R. Donald
622 Bruce Poulter
623 Dr Michael Holwill
624 Stephen J. Hounsham
625 Miss Rita Diprose
626 Peter Wright
627 Mrs H.C. Neill
628 Miss B.P. Deverell
629 Dora Bailey
630 Ralph Baber
631 George C. & Berta H. Bennett
632 Dr Peter J. Black
633 John Glanville Clark
634 P.J. Attewell
635 Mrs Mavis Priestley
636 CERL Wildlife Group
637 Mrs J. Jelley
638 R.I. & J.D. Silsby
639 Alison Morgan
640 D. McClintock
641 A. Marlow
642 J.M. & B.A. Keeley
643 R.B. Hastings
644 Ann Mellor
645 Mrs Felicity Ingram
646 Anne L. Robertson
647 D. Greig
648
649 M.J. Kelly
650 M. Harding
651 A.R.J. Paine
652 J.E.D. Milner
653 T.J. Bellamy
654 Giles Udy
655 Miss G.M. Tame
656 A.G. Gillham
657 R.H. Plumb
658 W.R. Downes
659 A. Trubshaw
660 Geoffrey Chandler
661 D.J. Turk
662 Mrs E.J.R. Simmonds
663 S.P. Croucher
664 Donald Islay Campbell
665 Elizabeth de Quidt
666 A.R.C. Hobbs

667 Dr P.A. Mayes
668 Dr Alan Behn
669 Mrs S.G. Beresford
670 F.S. Dobson
671 Miss P. Evans
672 Mrs H. Davoll
673 Helen Ballard
674 Stella Ruth Bridson
675 William John Hinde Smith
676 Philip E. Jones
677 Faith M. Speller
678 O.W. Wilmot
679 Richard Kelsall
680 R.D. Everington
681 Wilfred J. King
682 Annemarie Boettcher
683 Eunice Mary Elliott
684 H.J.W. Cleeve
685 Mr & Mrs D.G. Colman
686 Geraint Roberts
687 Michael John Bew
688 Robert Paul Goulding
689 A.J. Beale
690 Pamela M. Day
691 Norman Hiles
692 Marguerite Brinkley
693 Joyce & Robert Aspland
694 Frances Bigg
695 Mrs Jane Diggle
696
697 Mrs E.J. Dray
698
700 Mrs C. Bird
701 Haselemere Educational Museum
702 Dr and Mrs L.L. Ware
703 R. Furlonger
704 E.E. Orchard
705 Rosemary Steel
706 John F. Biden
707 F. Brocklehurst
708 Mrs P.M. Grover
709 I.S. Fentiman
710 Miss M.J. Tickner
711 Dr R.G. Davies
712 Joan Lay
713 M.E. Goring Dalton
714 I.J. Harnett
715 G.B. Rawinsky
716 John Bonavia
717 J. Richard Greenwell
718 Andrew Newman
Remaining names unlisted

ENDPAPERS: Surrey Reserves and sites of interest. (RST)

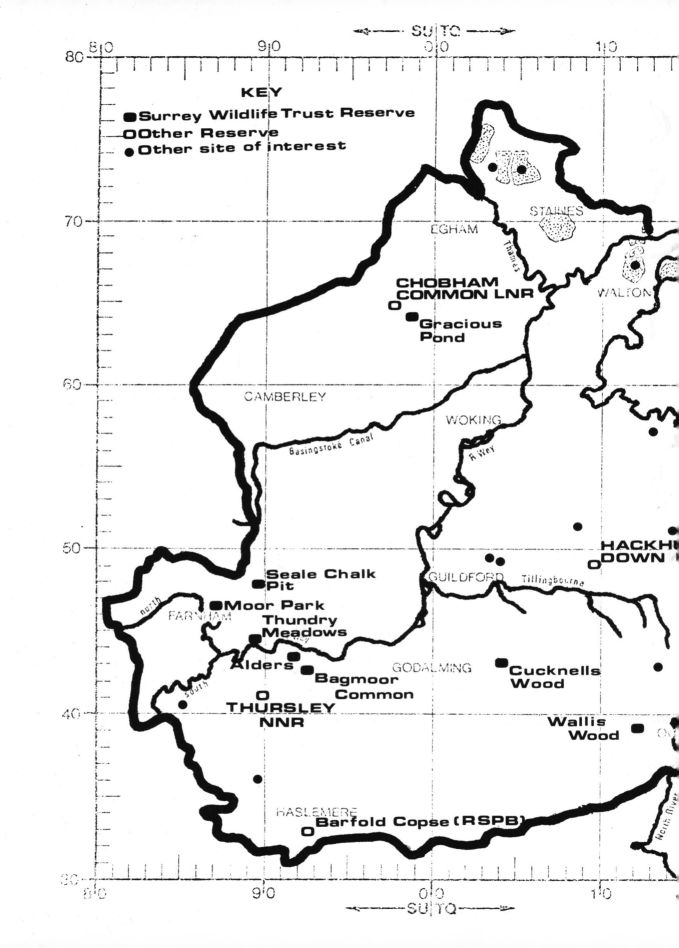